Laying the Foundations

A practical guide to sex and relationships education in primary schools

Second edition

Anna Martinez, Vanessa Cooper and Jane Lees

The Sex Education Forum is the national authority on sex and relationships education (SRE). It is a unique collaboration of over 90 member organisations and 750 practitioners with representatives from health, education, faith, disability and children's organisations. We believe that all children and young people have the right to good SRE and aim to provide all professionals involved in SRE with the information they need to ensure this right.

If you work with young people, in school or in a youth or community setting as a teacher, health professional, social worker or you are a parent or carer we can help provide you with the information and support you need to provide effective sex and relationships education. We work with teachers and health professionals across all settings promoting good practice through a range of publications and factsheets. If you have a query or need more information about any aspect of SRE you can e-mail us at sexedforum@ncb.org.uk or visit www.ncb.org.uk/sef.

NCB's vision is of a society in which children and young people contribute, are valued, and their rights respected. Our mission is to improve children and young people's experiences and life chances, reducing the impact of inequalities. NCB aims to:

- reduce inequalities of opportunity in childhood
- ensure children and young people can use their voice to improve their lives and the lives of those around them
- improve perceptions of children and young people
- enhance the health, learning, experiences and opportunities of children and young people
- encourage the building of positive and supportive relationships for children and young people with families, carers, friends and communities
- provide leadership through the use of evidence and research to improve policy and practice.

NCB has adopted and works within the UN Convention on the Rights of the Child.

Published by NCB

NCB, 8 Wakley Street, London EC1V 7QE
Tel: 020 7843 6000
Website: www.ncb.org.uk
Registered charity number: 258825

NCB works in partnership with Children in Scotland (www.childreninscotland.org.uk) and Children in Wales (www.childreninwales.org.uk).

Second edition
First edition published 2006

ISBN: 978 1 907969 51 5

British Library Cataloguing in Publication Data

A catalogue record for this book is available from the British Library

Typeset by Saxon Graphics Ltd, Derby
Printed by Hobbs the Printers, Totton, Southampton

Contents

Acknowledgements

First edition

This resource has been developed over a number of years with contributions from a range of projects – all of which have been funded by the Department for Education and Skills (DfES) and the Department of Health (DH). Contributions were made by: Janine Jolly, Caroline Ray, Sarah Thistle, Liz Swinden, Gill Frances and Simon Blake. It was edited by Anna Martinez and Vanessa Cooper.

We would like to thank the children in Redbridge, Bournemouth, Tower Hamlets and across England who talked with us about their sex and relationships education and helped shape this resource. Many thanks to all those who have contributed to its development: Nick Boddington, Jan Clarke, Lynwen Jones, Clare Smith, Dilys Went, Celine Andrews, Janet Sheehan, Peter Griffiths, David Lankshear, Heather White, Georgia Livingstone, Siobhann Rowland and Debbie Harris.

Second edition

We would like to thank Sam Beal, Isabel Reid and Sarah Jackson. Many thanks to Michelle Akarsu, Deputy Head of Chestnuts Primary School, Haringey, along with the staff and parents of the school for their contributions.

This edition contains an expanded section of lesson plans. The variety of activities included in these lesson plans represent good, current practice in SRE teaching, and have been drawn from many sources and the experience of many practitioners. The Extended Role Play activity cited in the Theme 3 lesson: Trust and Empathy was devised by Sue Plant.

In memory of Vanessa Cooper, co-author of the first edition of this publication, and a dedicated advocate for children's health and well-being.

Preface

The first edition of *Laying the Foundations* was based on the findings from a range of projects undertaken by the Sex Education Forum (SEF). In 1999–2000, SEF gathered information on sex and relationships education (SRE) practice through a mapping exercise and consultation process with primary schools in eight local education authorities (LEAs). In addition, questionnaires were sent to LEA advisors, healthy schools coordinators, teenage pregnancy coordinators and health promotion specialists to ascertain the level of support available to primary schools. SEF also talked to children in Key Stages 1 and 2, teachers and other professionals who support SRE in primary schools.

SEF found that many primary schools have successfully established SRE as part of personal, social, health and economic (PSHE) education and citizenship within a whole-school approach. What we learnt from them has helped us to understand how good quality education on relationships and sex is key to laying the early foundations for emotional and social development as well as for future work on sexual health. This resource builds on the excellent practice we have witnessed and is informed throughout by the voices of children, their teachers and a range of other adults from the wider community, including parents and carers.

This second edition aims to reflect how our understanding of SRE has developed in recent years. The profile of SRE in the primary curriculum has been raised by national reviews of SRE and PSHE, as well as by the successful Teenage Pregnancy Strategy that encouraged primary schools to teach SRE. Many teachers have been trained to teach SRE through the national PSHE CPD programme, which set standards for delivery. Widespread awareness of the earlier onset of puberty and concern about the sexualisation of children have also played a part. All of this has generated more demand for guidance on how schools can provide good quality SRE and what should be taught at each stage.

In response, this edition provides more guidance about involving children and their parents/carers in developing the SRE policy and programme and ensuring it meets their needs. There is also greater emphasis on assessment of learning as part of PSHE education, as recommended by Ofsted. The sample lesson plans have been expanded to suggest what a comprehensive programme of SRE should cover during the primary school years, and the range of activities in these lesson plans represent best practice.

Introduction

SRE starts on day one in every primary school, whether the school acknowledges it or not. I can't imagine that there is a reception class in this country where the teacher isn't helping the new pupils to build their confidence and self-esteem, recognise and manage their feelings, play and work cooperatively together, and understand and treat each other with respect. This work is absolutely key to helping children develop healthy relationships both now and in the future.

(Primary school teacher)

Children start learning about relationships, gender and sexuality at a very young age. As soon as they are born they begin to learn about relationships through the experience of interacting with the significant people in their lives, such as parents, carers, siblings, grandparents and later on with other children and staff at toddler groups, playgroups and nurseries. Some of these experiences will be positive, some negative.

Often children will have learnt about some of the differences between girls' and boys' and men's and women's bodies through, for example, seeing themselves and other members of the family naked, seeing others in the changing room at the local swimming pool, watching babies having their nappies changed, and through images on the television. Questions such as 'Where do babies come from?' are common at the age of three to five years, and many parents will have used this opportunity and others to provide simple age-appropriate explanations.

Comprehensive education on sex and relationships taught as part of broader personal, social, health and economic (PSHE) education in primary schools needs to build on children's preschool experiences and learning, not only of gender differences but also of gender similarities, relationships and feelings. The early years are a time of discovery, by providing a developmental programme, which starts in the Reception Year and builds as they move through the school to Year 6, teachers can help children make sense of what they see, hear and feel. Effective and early SRE lays vital foundations for future learning because it involves the development of the personal and social skills necessary for positive, healthy relationships. This includes developing empathy for others; caring and helping others; listening, taking turns and sharing. It also prepares children for the changes they will experience at puberty and gives them the confidence and skills to be able to talk to adults and ask for help.

Teachers and families must not shy away from these topics; by not talking openly and honestly, children will be receiving mixed messages. On the one hand, children are seeing that sex and relationships are everywhere, but on the other, they are getting the message that they are not something that adults want to talk about.

This resource will enable staff to develop their SRE policy and practice. It defines SRE within a PSHE education framework and whole-school approach, highlights the importance of SRE, and outlines relevant legislation and guidance. It provides ideas that can be adapted according to the needs and values framework of each individual primary school. It is accepted good practice to deliver the biological, social and emotional aspects of SRE together, and this resource deliberately brings all these aspects into one programme. Combining all aspects of SRE also reflects the expressed wishes of parents, carers and children.

Why teach SRE?

1

Why teach SRE?

What is SRE in primary schools?

Sex and relationships education (SRE) is learning about the emotional, social and physical aspects of growing up, relationships, sex, human sexuality and sexual health. It should equip children and young people with the information, skills and values to have safe, fulfilling and enjoyable relationships, and to take responsibility for their sexual health and well-being (SEF 2010).

In primary schools SRE specifically focuses on learning about our bodies, reproduction and puberty within the context of emotions, relationships, healthy choices and equality. It also includes family, friendships and feelings. This early learning lays the foundations for future work on sexual and reproductive health and so helps to prepare children for adulthood. It contributes to the emotional and social development of children, helps them to develop a secure sense of identity and to function well in the world.

SRE is an integral element of the planned programme of study for personal, social, health and economic (PSHE) education. In an integrated programme, the PSHE education curriculum also covers emotional health and well-being, drugs, healthy eating and physical activity, citizenship and safety. The self-esteem, skills and emotional intelligence required to make healthy choices underpin all these topics, and it is therefore essential and good practice that teaching and learning about sex and relationships is planned and implemented within this broader framework rather than as a stand-alone subject.

> I'm glad that someone had the idea of sex education because now I properly understand internal and external changes in our bodies. Now I can keep this information to help me cope when I get older and explain it to my children.
> Year 5 girl

SRE terminology

> My son was in Year 2 at the time. It was such a shock that they was gonna be teaching my six-year-old son sex education. I think other parents were all the same to start with because it's the word 'sex' and six-year-old kids – it doesn't go together does it? But when I got a chance to see the video I realised the way they were doing it was so constructive … realised it wasn't about the actual sex side of it, it was about giving the children an insight into what the future holds sort of thing.
>
> (Parent)

Many primary schools, particularly at Key Stage 1, use different terminology to describe the sex and relationships elements of PSHE education – such as growing up, our bodies, my family, my body, caring for others, keeping clean, and keeping safe. Whatever it is called, primary schools certainly recognise the vital role they play in building on the learning established within the home and early years settings, and in laying the foundations for more detailed SRE at Key Stage 2 and later on in secondary school. For example, learning about washing hands and sneezing into a tissue lays the foundation for much later work on protecting ourselves and others from infections, including sexually transmitted infections.

Children's wishes and needs

Childhood is a time of discovery and learning and children frequently tell us how much they value SRE to help them make sense of their changing world. However, they also say that it is often 'too little, too late and too biological'. Children want opportunities to learn about and discuss the emotional and practical aspects of puberty and growing up – what to expect and how to cope – not simply the biological and reproductive information. It is also vital they are prepared for these changes before they begin puberty, and that it is not left until Year 6, by which time many children, particularly girls, have already started this transition. Preparation for puberty should begin in Years 3 and 4 because it is not uncommon for girls to start menstruating at this age, or to show other signs of puberty.

Children are also exposed, through the range of media, to far more information about sex and relationships than ever before. Children pick up lots of ideas and images from the media, some positive and some negative, and need support to make sense of them. In 2010 the Home Office published an independent review looking at sexualisation of children as part of the government strategy to end violence against women and girls. The review acknowledged difficulties in measuring the impact of sexualisation on children's long-term development, but found: 'broad agreement among researchers and experts in health and welfare that sexualising children prematurely places them at risk of a variety of harms, ranging from body image disturbances to being victims of abuse and sexual violence' (Papadopoulos 2010: 74).

The Sex Education Forum (SEF) believes that good quality SRE has a key role to play in protecting children and young people from sexualisation by providing:

- a safe source of accurate and balanced information about physical, emotional and social development, as well as legal and health facts
- nurturing core values of equality and mutual respect
- skills development such as communication, confidence to resist pressure and critical thinking.

Therefore, SRE provides children with an opportunity to have their questions answered, misinformation corrected and fears allayed.

Parents' and carers' expectations and the need for support

From my point of view as a parent it opened the subject up for me. The children actually come home and ask questions and it's a lot easier for me to answer than bringing it up. I never got sex education because my parents wouldn't bring the subject up. It's them bringing it up with us that makes it a lot easier to open the conversation up.

(Parent)

The vast majority of parents and carers want their children to receive school-based SRE (fpa/Mori 2000; SEF 2006). In a recent mumsnet Survey (2011) 98 per cent of parents said they were happy for their children to attend school SRE lessons. Although there is a parental right to withdraw children from the non-National Curriculum elements of SRE, less than 1 per cent choose to do so (Ofsted 2002). In many cases the decision reflects a misunderstanding of the purpose of the programme. For some, school-based SRE provides reinforcement of the messages provided at home; for others, who feel embarrassed and unsure about how to talk to their children, it can provide an opportunity to start discussions in the home. (For more information on how to involve parents see the Involving parents and carers 'Establishing needs' section on page 16.)

> It is helpful for children my age to understand going through puberty. I think I'm calmer now I know what my body is doing and I think my friends are calmer as well.
> Year 5 girl

SRE supports the emotional and social development of children

There is growing recognition that a child's emotional and social well-being affects their ability to learn, and that children who are anxious, angry or depressed will find it hard to learn (Goleman 1995). Relationships with others also affect an individual's emotional state, and children and young people who are having problems with relationships at home or at school are likely to be in a highly charged emotional state.

Schools therefore have a major role to play in their pupils' emotional and social development in order to enable them to learn and to achieve. Schools also need to pay attention to creating an inclusive environment that supports all children – including those with social and behavioural difficulties.

Quality SRE and PSHE education that explores the following themes will support a child's social and emotional development:

- empathy
- self-awareness
- motivation
- social skills
- managing feelings.

There are a range of materials and websites designed to help schools work on social and emotional development, such as social and emotional aspects of learning (SEAL) (DfES 2005), currently available at http://www.teachfind.com.

The whole-school approach

Children learn from what is explicitly taught in the classroom, from their day-to-day experiences and observations around the school, and how they relate to each other. To ensure that these experiences do not undermine the messages in formal SRE, primary schools need to ensure that there are consistent messages about relationships, health, sex and sexuality. To achieve this it is important that a whole-school approach is taken. The following checklist outlines structures and policies that should be in place across a whole school community in order to support effective SRE.

Checklist for a whole-school approach

☐ **Leadership, management and managing change.** The school leadership should understand and value the importance of SRE to children's health and well-being, and should support a safe and positive climate for its delivery within the curriculum.

☐ **Policy development.** Schools should have a SRE/PSHE education policy in place, developed in consultation with children, parents/carers, staff, governors and the community. All school policies should specifically address how the school intends to meet the needs of all children, and how staff respond to questions relating to SRE.

☐ **Curriculum planning and resourcing SRE/PSHE education.** There should be a dedicated weekly time slot, and learning should be reinforced across other elements of the curriculum such as literacy, ICT, science and technology. Resources used within the curriculum should be carefully chosen, should be age- and maturity-appropriate, and reflect the local community.

☐ **Teaching and learning.** Teachers should be familiar with, and competent to use, a range of teaching and learning techniques including active participatory learning methods.

☐ **School culture and environment.** The grounds, buildings and rooms should be welcoming and secure, and this positive and friendly atmosphere should be reflected in school publications and handouts. The environment should reflect the core values of SRE by, for example, showing a range of girls, boys and family types engaged in non-stereotypical activities.

☐ **Giving pupils a voice.** Pupils should be included in all aspects of school life, such as being involved in reviewing and developing policies, and in evaluating the SRE programme.

☐ **Provision of pupil support services.** It is vital for all children and young people in the school to be able to access support and advice services. Partnership working with local agencies will facilitate this. Supplies and disposal of sanitary products should be made easily accessible to girls.

☐ **Staff professional development, health and well-being.** School staff need professional development in SRE/PSHE education and ongoing support and supervision.

☐ **Partnerships with parents, carers and local communities.** It is important to liaise regularly with parents and carers to establish a link between home and school, and to involve them in decision making. Particular attempts should be made to explore issues related to SRE with parents and carers from a range of faith backgrounds.

☐ **Assessing, recording and reporting pupils' achievements.** Assessment is vital in order to check learning and understanding of the subject, to get to know the children, to celebrate their successes and build on what's working well.

Adapted from the National Healthy Schools Programme (Department of Health 2005).

The law on SRE

This section summarises current legislation affecting teaching about sex and relationships in maintained schools.

The law relating to SRE content

- Schools are required to develop a curriculum that: 'Promotes the spiritual, moral, cultural, mental and physical development of pupils at school and of society; and prepares pupils for the opportunities, responsibilities and experiences of adult life' (National Curriculum, currently under review).
- The biological elements of SRE, including puberty and reproduction as set out in the National Curriculum Science Order, are mandatory for all pupils.
- Children and young people should learn about the nature of marriage and its importance for family life and the bringing up of children.
- Teaching and materials should be appropriate and have regard to the age and the religious and cultural background of the pupils concerned.

The law relating to SRE policy

- All schools must provide an up-to-date policy that describes the content and organisation of any SRE provided outside the National Curriculum Science Order. It is the school governors' responsibility to ensure that the policy is developed and implemented.
- Primary schools should have a policy statement that describes the SRE provided, or that gives a statement of the decision not to provide SRE other than that provided in the National Curriculum Science Order.
- Secondary schools are required to provide an SRE programme that includes (as a minimum) information about sexually transmitted infections and HIV/AIDS.
- It is the responsibility of a school's governing body to ensure that the policy is made available to parents.
- Parents have a right to withdraw their children (until the age of 19) from any school SRE taught outside the Science Curriculum (for more information, see the 'Parental right to withdrawal' page 18).
- Schools have a legal duty to ensure the well-being of their pupils, and SRE contributes to this duty.
- Governing bodies must have due regard to any SRE Guidance issued by the Secretary of State.

Education Reform Act 1988, Education Act 1996, Learning and Skills Act 2000 and Education and Inspections Act 2006

Sex and Relationship Education Guidance (2000)

Current SRE Guidance aims to support schools in developing SRE, and school governors are required to have regard to this guidance. The Guidance recommends strongly that all primary schools 'should have a sex and relationship education programme tailored to the age and the physical and emotional maturity of the children. It should ensure that both boys and girls know about puberty and how a baby is born – as set out in Key Stages 1 and 2 of the National Science Curriculum.' (At the time of writing the National Curriculum is also under review, with a revised version scheduled for September 2013.)

The Guidance also states that 'all children … need to know about puberty before they experience the onset of physical changes. In the early primary school years, education about relationships needs to focus upon friendships, bullying and the building of self-esteem.' The Guidance goes on to provide that SRE in primary schools should ensure that all pupils:

- develop confidence in talking, listening and thinking about feelings and relationships
- are able to name parts of the body and describe how their bodies work
- can protect themselves, ask for help and support, and are prepared for puberty.

(DfEE 2000, under review at the time of writing)

Sexual Offences Act 2003
This Act aims to clarify what constitutes a crime of a sexual nature against children, young people and adults. The Act does not limit children's entitlement to SRE. Staff giving information or advice with the purpose of protecting a child from pregnancy, STIs, protecting their physical safety or promoting their well-being, are protected under the Act.

Equality Act 2010 and SRE
Schools must have due regard to the need to:

- Eliminate unlawful discrimination, harassment and victimisation and any other conduct that is unlawful under the Equality Act, with reference to age (only in employment), disability, pregnancy and maternity, religion or belief, race, sex, sexual orientation, gender reassignment, and marriage and civil partnerships.
- Advance equality of opportunity.
- Foster good relations.

The Equality Act 2010 therefore applies to the way the curriculum is delivered, as schools and other education providers must ensure that issues are taught in a way that does not subject pupils to discrimination. It is also a legal requirement for schools to teach a balanced view of any political issue. Schools must ensure equal opportunities in the education they provide, so it would not be lawful for schools to provide SRE only for girls or only for boys. SRE should cover equality and diversity within relationships, gender equality, family diversity and be sensitive to different faith perspectives.

Ofsted Framework 2012

All primary schools are inspected by Office for Standards in Education (Ofsted), including academies and free schools. PSHE education, which includes SRE, is expected to meet the same high standards required by Ofsted of all subjects and teaching. Teachers must have consistently high expectations of all pupils, draw on excellent subject knowledge, plan astutely, set challenging tasks based upon an accurate assessment of pupils' prior skills, knowledge and understanding, and use well-judged and imaginative teaching strategies.

The Ofsted Framework is clear in stating that the most important role of teaching is to raise achievement, and that teaching has an important role in promoting the pupils' spiritual, moral, social and cultural development.

Inspections must consider:

- Pupils' behaviour towards, and respect for, other young people and adults, including freedom from bullying and harassment, cyberbullying and prejudice-based bullying.
- The focus on behaviour will also include pupils' attitudes to learning, their conduct in lessons and around school.
- Pupils' ability to assess and manage risk appropriately and keep themselves safe. Risk includes those risks associated with extremism, new technology, substance misuse, knives and gangs, relationships (including sexual relationships), water, fire, roads and railways.
- Whether the school provides a broad and balanced curriculum that promotes pupils' good behaviour and safety and their spiritual, moral, social and cultural development.
- Whether the school engages with parents in supporting pupil achievement, behaviour and safety, and their spiritual, moral, social and cultural development.

In respect of 'overall effectiveness', inspections must consider how well the school provides positive experiences for all pupils by promoting their spiritual, moral, social and cultural development through planned and coherent opportunities in the curriculum and through interactions with teachers and other adults (PSHE Association 2012).

Groups of pupils
Inspection is primarily about evaluating how individual pupils benefit from their school. It is important to test the school's response to individual needs by observing how well it helps all pupils to make progress and fulfil their potential, especially those whose needs, dispositions, aptitudes or circumstances require particularly perceptive and expert teaching and, in some cases, additional support. Depending on the type of school, such pupils may include: disabled pupils; boys; girls; lesbian, gay and bisexual pupils; transgender pupils; groups of pupils whose prior attainment may be different from that of other groups; those who are academically more or less able; pupils for whom English is an additional language; minority ethnic pupils; Gypsy, Roma and Traveller children; looked after children; pupils known to be eligible for free school meals; young carers; pupils from low income backgrounds; and other vulnerable groups.

Academies and free schools
Each academy and free school will have an individual funding agreement outlining what they will teach. It is nevertheless good practice for all schools to have an SRE policy that is developed in consultation with pupils and parents/carers. All schools, including academies and free schools, are still required to work within the Equalities Act 2010, are inspected by Ofsted and must take due regard of any guidance issued by the Secretary of State.

Academies have been encouraged to use a 'model funding agreement' (available at www.education.gov.uk). In terms of SRE, this model funding agreement states that academies must: 'Have regard to any Guidance issued by the Secretary of State on Sex and Relationships Education to ensure that children are protected from inappropriate teaching materials and they learn the nature of marriage and its importance for family life and for bringing up children.' The current applicable Guidance is the *Sex and Relationships Education Guidance* (DfEE 2000).

The other curriculum obligations in the model funding agreement are that academies must teach English, mathematics and science, and must make provision for the teaching of religious education.

Developing and reviewing SRE policy

2

Developing and reviewing SRE policy

All primary schools are required to have an up-to-date policy that outlines the provision of sex and relationships education. The current Guidance advises that the policy should be developed in consultation with children, parents, carers and the school community, and that it should form part of the school's PSHE policy (DfEE 2000). The SRE policy should take note of local and national health priorities and be reviewed and revised regularly (at least every three years). Once completed, it should be referred to in the school prospectus and made available to pupils, parents and staff via the school website and/or intranet. (See the accompanying flow chart – 'Process for the development or review of an SRE policy' – which maps out issues that schools need to consider.)

Process for the development or review of an SRE policy

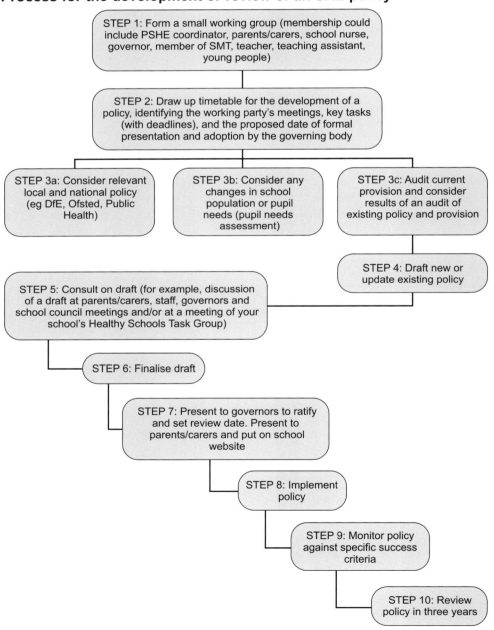

> Governors need to be confident they understand what is involved.
> Headteacher

Establishing a working group

A working party was established that included the head and deputy head, school nurse, health promotion specialist, parents, parent governor, parent/associate staff and priest. The working group discussed and developed common aims and objectives, which enabled the policy and programme to be developed. As a result, SRE is now taught throughout the school from Reception to Year 6. This is ensuring that the children can develop their ideas slowly and carefully. SRE is coordinated by the deputy head in close cooperation with a senior teacher from the infants' department.

(Headteacher, Roman Catholic school)

A working group to take responsibility for developing or reviewing the school's SRE policy should be established. Membership could include the PSHE education coordinator, a parent/carer, the school nurse, a governor, a member of the senior management team (SMT), a teacher, a teaching assistant and a pupil. This group will draw up a timetable for the development of a policy, identifying the working party's meetings, key tasks (with deadlines), and the proposed date of formal presentation and adoption by the governing body.

Role of governors

Responsibility for the SRE policy of a school ultimately lies with the governing body. Governors are an important resource in a school, and at least one representative of the governing body should be part of the working group that develops and reviews the policy and programme. Generally, governors receive little training on SRE and PSHE education, so schools should explore opportunities to include governors in whole-staff training sessions and discussions as often as is reasonably practical.

Auditing current provision

When developing or reviewing an SRE policy, it is important to ascertain current practice. Developing SRE is not about starting from scratch, but rather about consolidating and further strengthening existing work on friendships, family life, relationships, positive behaviour, growth and change. In reviewing the policy, schools will need to consider any changes to their school community or to the resourcing of the programme. For example, the school may recently have enriched their work on family diversity to reflect families with LGBT (lesbian, gay, bisexual and transgender) members, and the policy should reflect this.

Auditing tool
The auditing tool set out in the accompanying table is designed to collect information on what is working well and can be built on, and what is not working so well and therefore indicates room for improvement. The PSHE education lead within the school should complete the audit in consultation with the working group and should involve, if appropriate, colleagues from the local education or health authority with interests in this area.

Auditing tool for SRE/PSHE policy development and revision

Aspects of school life	What happens at present?	Response	Action to be taken
Pupil consultation	• Does the school involve the children to ensure that the policy and programme meet their needs?		
Coordination	• Does the school have a PSHE and Citizenship coordinator? • Is this the person responsible for SRE? • Is there a named governor for SRE? • Is there a budget to support the development of SRE?		
Policy	• Does the school have an up-to-date SRE policy? • Is it part of the PSHE & Citizenship policy in line with the SRE Guidance (DfEE 2000)? • Does it address local and national policy initiatives? • Has it been successfully implemented? • Is it reviewed regularly (every two to three years)?		
Related school policies	• Are there other relevant policies and how are they linked? (Examples are: equal opportunities, anti-bullying, positive behaviour, child protection, confidentiality) • How are the policies communicated to children and parents/carers?		
Programme	• How is SRE currently delivered and to which year groups? • Who delivers it? • Are the staff responsible trained in SRE? • What resources are used? • Where else is SRE, in its broadest sense, covered? (Examples include: assembly, RE, science, literacy hour) • Does the programme ensure that pupils will reach the outcomes recommended by Ofsted? • How does SRE address the diverse needs of children in the school? • How do you know the programme meets their needs? • How do you answer questions about sex and relationships?		

Aspects of school life	What happens at present?	Response	Action to be taken
Parents and carers	• What mechanisms are in place for consulting with parents/carers? When are parents/carers invited in to school? • Is there support available for parents/carers, either directly or indirectly (for instance, the school nurse or leaflets) to help them talk to their children about puberty, sex and relationships? • Have any parents/carers withdrawn their children from SRE? • If so why? • How was this dealt with? • Is there alternative provision?		
In-service education and training (INSET)	• What SRE training have staff received? • What whole-staff INSET is provided in school? • What opportunities are there for the whole staff team to meet together to discuss SRE? • What training opportunities are there for non-teaching staff?		
Wider community	• Are outside visitors invited into school to contribute to the school SRE programme? • If yes, who are they? • Is there a protocol for the use of outside visitors?		
Whole-school	• What provision is available in school for girls who are menstruating? • Are there dispensers/disposal facilities? • How are protocols regarding acquiring supplies/accessing disposal facilities communicated to the children? • How are unexpected questions dealt with? • What pastoral care is available? • How is unacceptable language/behaviour challenged?		

Establishing needs

Involving children

Children already have certain ideas about relationships, sex and love they pick up from their friends and home. So giving them the chance to help design the programme to respond to the kinds of questions and concerns they have is really important. Then we know the lessons are relevant to them.

(Primary school teacher)

Example of practice

St Luke's Primary School in Brighton and Hove carries out pupil conferencing on an annual basis as part of the self-evaluation of PSHE education. This involves assessing the learning of a small group of pupils from each year group and asking them for their views of the school's programme.

Involving children in the development of policy and curriculum will help ensure their needs are met. Their involvement can take place in a variety of ways including needs assessment activities to establish what they want to learn about and evaluation of lessons at the end of a programme to find out how helpful the activities and resources were. 'Draw and write' and anonymous question boxes are excellent ways of establishing what children already know and what concerns or questions they have. (See section on Assessment of SRE page 41 for needs assessment activities.)

Surveys and questionnaires are also ways of linking SRE policy with other areas of the curriculum such as maths. School councils can be interviewed or invited to devise and undertake a survey of other children's views.

In order to evaluate existing SRE programmes, the following questions are useful to consider:

- Where do you get information about your body, growing up, relationships and feelings?
- Does what is taught in school at the moment answer all of your questions?
- What would you like more information on?
- Do you feel able to ask for support and advice?
- Do you feel confident talking about feelings and emotions?
- Do you feel safe to learn in SRE lessons?
- Do the activities used in lessons help you to learn?
- What do you think would improve SRE in our school?

For more information on involving children, see 'Let's Get It Right – A toolkit for involving primary school children in reviewing SRE' (SEF 2013).

If you have worked in a genuine partnership with parents – you've consulted them about the policy, made resources open to them – then they are very reassured and actually relieved. They will then support the work.
Governor advisor

I was really glad the school invited me in to see the resources and talk about what the children would be learning in sex education. I was worried that my son, who has special educational needs, wouldn't understand what was being taught, but I am now reassured that it is taught in a sensitive way.
Parent

Involving parents and carers

It is the responsibility of the governing body to ensure that parents are informed of the school's SRE policy. It is good practice to involve parents and carers from the outset in the development of the policy. Schools have a vital role in building partnerships with parents and carers to support children and young people in effective learning, and this includes SRE. Feedback from schools that have worked to build a strong partnership with parents and carers has shown significant benefit to pupil attainment and well-being. In addition, a school-based SRE programme is unlikely to meet the needs of pupils without input from parents/carers and the wider community.

Schools that have worked in partnership with parents and carers have found that this process helps to allay parents' fears about the content and purpose of SRE and, as one parent reported, 'Now I know what it's [SRE's] all about I'm not worried.' This has led to increased support for the schools' work in this area and a strengthening of the home–school relationship. Schools will need to ensure they make every effort to engage parents and carers from across the whole school community and they may need support from other services (such as those offering translation services) to do this.

Case study

Consulting with parents on SRE policy

A primary school in south-west London was reviewing its SRE or 'Growing up' policy and wanted to involve parents in their discussions. Separate meetings were planned to accommodate parents available during the daytime and those available only at the end of the working day. Also, a separate meeting was arranged for parents whose first language is not English, and four translators were employed to support the Urdu, Polish, Somalian and Pashtu speaking parents. The school has a sizeable Somalian community and so also had to take into account that men and women could not be in the same room when talking about this subject. The school was able to work round this by offering a meeting with the male headteacher at the same time that the women met with the female deputy head. Across the different meetings about 70 parents attended.

In one meeting they looked at the teaching resources, and interestingly some parents favoured more graphic (scientific) images over cartoons, as a way of ensuring that the children received the correct information. The school was impressed by the response to the meetings and the suggestions made about the content of the programme and the resources to be used. In response to the points raised the school is seeking to find resources that will be suitable for children and parents of the Muslim faith, and is also considering whether or not to introduce some of the themes to younger year groups as appropriate.

Many parents thanked the school for providing the opportunity to have a discussion about this topic and were pleased that the school was delivering this subject to their children. One parent said that they 'appreciate the school talking to parents about a topic that not everyone is comfortable with'.

There are various methods for consulting parents and carers on SRE policy, and a combination of methods may work best, such as:

- Emailing the entire draft policy out to all parents and carers, or posting the document on the school website and inviting feedback and comments.
- Emailing an edited parents' version of the policy, or posting the document on the school website and asking specific questions for parents to respond to. See Appendix I for an example of a parents questionnaire.
- Extending an open invitation to all parents via the school newsletter to a meeting about the policy, and using this as a forum to discuss the key content of the policy, focusing on the parts of the policy most likely to interest parents.
- Inviting all parents to a meeting, but then specifically targeting individual parents and carers by text, phone or email. For example, parents who you know work in health and would have expertise to contribute, parents who may have particular concerns about SRE or may have a particular perspective to offer. Coombe Road Primary School in Brighton and Hove, for instance, used the home school liaison worker from the Ethnic Minority Achievement Service to invite Bengali parents and carers to a meeting about the SRE policy and supported this consultation by translating for these parents at the meeting.
- Tasking a particular group of parents and carers with carrying out the consultation. For example, a table could be set up in the playground at 'home time' or during a parents'/carers' evening, with parents being asked about their views on SRE and the school policy.
- Involving pupils/students in asking their parents/carers for their views of SRE and the school policy, and feeding these back through the school council. Also, sharing outcomes from needs identification exercises or feedback from pupils with parents/carers, such as showing parents the questions children post anonymously in question boxes.

Parental right to withdrawal

Parents and carers have the right to withdraw their children from any SRE taught outside the statutory National Curriculum. However, parents and carers are not able to withdraw pupils from SRE that arises incidentally as part of any curriculum area, provided that such discussion is relatively limited.

Schools need to ensure that parents and carers are informed of and understand the right to withdraw their children from SRE, and how to exercise that right. The school SRE policy should contain information on the right to withdraw and the school should invite parents with concerns to discuss these issues so that any misunderstandings may be resolved. Some parents, for example, may misunderstand the aims and purpose of SRE and may be concerned about age appropriateness.

Routinely communicating with parents and carers about SRE and involving them in its development can pre-empt concern about the programme. Schools will need to make a particular effort to involve parents and carers from a range of faith backgrounds in these discussions. In the rare cases where certain parents and carers are opposing the programme it often works well to involve other parents and carers in exploring these concerns, perhaps at a meeting. Ultimately, however, schools will need to develop a language that acknowledges parental choice to withdraw and reveals a confidence that the school's programme is based on the needs of pupils and is in line with local data and national guidance.

Supporting parents and carers with SRE at home

SRE is the joint responsibility of parents/carers and the school. Parents and carers are key people in educating their children about sex and relationships, and in maintaining the culture and ethos of their family. This includes helping their children cope with the emotional and physical aspects of growing up and in preparing them for the challenges and responsibilities that sexual maturity brings. Many parents and carers find it difficult to talk to their children about sex and relationships and appreciate support in this aspect of their role.

Parents and carers report that they want to know when and how SRE is being taught so that they can follow up with their children at home. Good practice is to keep parents and carers informed of what is being taught in PSHE education and SRE as they would other subject areas. Resources used in the programme or picture books from the school library can be lent to parents so they can reinforce learning at home. Curriculum evenings provide an ideal opportunity to show parents and carers materials used and to display children's work in PSHE education in the same way as for other subjects. Teachers have found that sharing children's views of the SRE programme and their concerns about growing up, alongside demonstrations of active learning methods, provides a much more positive and helpful experience for parents and carers. (See Appendix 1 for a sample letter to parents and carers that could be inserted in a newsletter and/or sent and emailed to parents and carers.) For more information on supporting parents see page 32 in Chapter 3.

For more information on involving parents in SRE see 'Let's work together – A practical guide for schools to involve parents and carers in SRE' (SEF 2013).

Case study

'Pre-view': Supporting parents project
The 'Pre-view' Project in Hillingdon was originally developed with two primary schools in order to engage parents in identifying books for the schools' libraries. The process enabled parental participation in reading and assessment of materials and also provided opportunities to discuss the issues raised in informal learning groups. Supported by a specialist health advisor, the approach creates a climate in which parents are able to gain confidence in discussing SRE issues with their children within the context of a wider understanding of PSHE education. The experience of the parents is used to inform the development of SRE/PSHE work in the school and the procurement of relevant materials by the Schools' Library Service.

This project improved parental/school engagement and informed selection of SRE/PSHE learning resources. Additionally, it helped raise parental confidence in relating to their children on issues addressed by the SRE/PSHE curricula and on issues raised by children.

Writing the policy

Once the consultation and audit have been completed, the working group can discuss the results and start developing or reviewing the SRE policy. Some schools have stand-alone SRE policies, although others combine their SRE policy with their PSHE education policy (while ensuring there is enough detail to support the effective delivery of SRE). The purpose of a PSHE education policy with an SRE element is to:

- ensure that staff are aware of what the school will deliver and how it will be done
- clarify those values that underpin PSHE education/SRE, and that form part of the school's ethos emphasising children's entitlement
- provide a tool to inform parents and carers about PSHE education and SRE
- create a starting point for staff to receive training, support and resources
- ensure links with pastoral care.

A policy framework

The framework for PSHE education with an integrated SRE policy shown in the text box can be used for developing a policy at your school. It describes the basic information that should be included.

A policy framework for PSHE education that includes SRE

1. Introduction
- Name of school
- Date policy was completed
- Person responsible
- How the policy was formulated
- Review date
- Links to other relevant policies, such as teaching and learning, anti-bullying and equalities
- Who will receive a copy of the policy and how it will be made available

2. Information about ...
The school and community and the important role that PSHE education including SRE plays in the school curriculum. How provision is supported by the whole-school ethos.

3. Statement of values
How PSHE education (and SRE as part of this) supports the ethos of the school and what the values that underpin the programme are. For example, SRE supports the values of the school by promoting children's self-esteem and emotional well-being, helping them to form and maintain worthwhile and satisfying relationships based on respect for themselves and for others, at home, school, work and in the community.

4. The objectives for PSHE education (including SRE)

What pupils will have learned by the end of each Key Stage, including topics and themes such as SRE, social and emotional aspects of learning (SEAL), emotional health and well-being, healthy eating, exercise, drug education, safety and citizenship. How PSHE education contributes to Healthy School and other practice such as anti-bullying.

5. Organisation and planning

- Name of PSHE education coordinator and lead governor
- Who teaches PSHE education
- How PSHE education will meet the needs of all children including those with special educational needs
- What the specific arrangements are for special educational needs and disabled children (timetabling, resources, staffing and revision)
- Where PSHE education is taught (for example, how it forms part of the curriculum)
- Criteria for resources selection
- Staff professional development and support
- How to link to, and make pupils aware of, the pastoral systems and health advisory service in school and the wider community.

6. Teaching and learning

- Needs assessment
- Active teaching and learning methods
- Pupil groupings
- Creating a safe environment for learning and teaching
- Confidentiality
- Guidance on answering questions
- Ensuring pupil participation and active citizenship, including peer education
- Ensuring partnerships across school with parents and the wider community, including agreements for using visitors in the classroom
- Assessment and reporting on progress
- Evaluation.

7. Specific issues related to SRE

What good practice in SRE amounts to, integrating the biological, social and emotional elements; needs-based; and participatory education. Legal aspects relating to SRE should also be covered, including the parental right to withdraw, National Curriculum Science and PSHE Guidance (see 'The law on SRE' section in Chapter 1). How the school supports specific needs of girls and boys will also be included (for example, sanitary provision, and providing a positive role model for boys and those with gender identity issues) and how the school deals with specific issues, including answering questions, managing disclosures, and challenging inappropriate comments and behaviours such as gender stereotyping, sexism, homophobia and transphobia.

8. Monitoring and evaluation
Covering who will monitor the implementation of the policy, how the work will be evaluated and when it will be next reviewed (every two to three years is advisable).

9. Appendices
More detailed guidance on specific issues related to SRE can be placed in the appendices.

Specific issues for consideration

Personal disclosures and safeguarding
Children may make personal disclosures, particularly within SRE where an atmosphere of trust is created and sensitive topics are discussed. Teachers and others supporting SRE, including outside visitors, cannot offer or guarantee absolute confidentiality. If a pupil directly makes a disclosure about sexual activity, exploitation or abuse, child protection/safeguarding procedures must be followed. Teachers and other adults working in schools must be absolutely clear about the boundaries of their legal and professional roles and responsibilities if disclosures are made (and should refer to their local Safeguarding/Child Protection Guidance).

A clear and explicit position on dealing with personal disclosures should be included within the SRE policy. This should ensure good practice throughout the school and it is important that all the key groups – staff, pupils and parents – understand the policy, and schools need to ensure that every effort has been made to inform them of it. The position statement should:

- set out clear procedures for staff to follow
- emphasise the importance of using a working agreement in lessons, which lays down ground rules
- make sure that pupils and parents or carers are aware of the school's policy on dealing with disclosures and how it works in practice
- reassure pupils that their best interests will be supported
- encourage pupils to talk to their parents or carers and giving them support to do so.

For more practical guidance on personal disclosures in a class room setting see **Dealing with personal disclosures** page 37. All staff must ensure that they are familiar with their school's child protection/ safeguarding policy and procedures.

Gender
The SRE policy will need to consider gender issues, and how the differing needs of boys and girls will be addressed from both within and beyond the formal SRE curriculum.

Gender stereotyping begins at an early age and limits both genders. If these stereotypes go unchallenged, they can also result in bullying for those children who choose to step outside 'expected gender roles': for

> I was scared to talk about it as it is one of those things you are ashamed to talk about with your mates. But I know it is easier to talk to them having seen the film.
> Year 6 boy

> Before the programme I was worried about getting my period, but now I realise it is all a fact of life.
> Year 6 girl

example, boys who don't like football; girls who prefer trains to dolls. How to combat prejudice and stereotypes and deal positively with difference is a key issue for children and their teachers, and this should be included in the SRE policy, perhaps by giving examples of how the school aims to address the issues on a day-to-day basis.

One of the aims of SRE must be to open up communication between genders and to improve mutual understanding. Researchers believe that the Dutch experience, where young people are much more at ease discussing sexual matters with a member of the opposite sex, stems from childhood, where children play in mixed gender groups (Ingham and van Zessen 1998). This is much less common in the UK, where children often split into single gender friendship groups at an early age. A whole-school approach that supports children playing together and also learning from each other could do much to improve relationship skills.

Although there are common skills and knowledge that both girls and boys will need, both genders have differing needs. It is also important that school staff are sensitive to the specific transitions and critical moments in puberty and that appropriate arrangements are made for pastoral care.

Boys
In general, boys receive less sex and relationships education from their families. Boys also report that formal school SRE seems to be about girls and for girls, and that little attention is paid to their needs. Some female teachers report feeling less confident dealing with pubertal development of boys compared with puberty in girls. Accurate information about the physical and emotional changes that take place at puberty is extremely important. Both boys and girls should have a basic knowledge of what happens to each gender.

Boys also need to be prepared for the specific changes they will experience through puberty. Boys report that their preparation for puberty is often limited to information on voice-breaking. They would also like advice and support with regard to other aspects of puberty, such as wet dreams; growing facial hair and shaving; and reassurance about what is 'normal' in terms of development, penis size and uncontrollable erections. Many primary schools invite a father, male nurse or male youth worker to join a lesson in order to support the boys and answer their questions.

Girls
Many girls are not prepared for the onset of puberty despite having some awareness of periods from adverts on the TV, in shops, public toilets, overheard conversations and stories from older sisters and relatives. Adequate preparation will help them to make sense of these bits of information that might otherwise be misleading or negative. How we do this carries significant messages, both about how we value them as girls now, and about their transition into adult womanhood.

Lack of appropriate school facilities for girls coping with menstruation in primary school may also damage their sense of pride in themselves and their bodies. Primary schools need to make adequate arrangements to help girls cope with menstruation at school, which might include providing sanitary disposal facilities in each toilet cubicle for older pupils and preparing all staff (including non-teaching staff) to deal with requests for sanitary towels in a helpful manner and without embarrassment. Extra support will be necessary for those girls who are early starters. Early negative experiences, such as unexpected bleeding, difficulties in obtaining sanitary supplies and teasing from other children, can have a damaging effect on girls' self-esteem.

Gender identity
Primary school communities will routinely include children with gender identity issues. For example, a biologically born boy who identifies as a girl or vice versa. Gender identity issues in infancy, childhood and adolescence are complex and have varied causes. Whatever the cause, a child with a gender identity problem may be unhappy, and their ability to learn may suffer as a result. Primary schools need to accept children with gender identity issues unconditionally for the people they are, show a genuine interest in them and protect them from any nastiness or bullying. Schools will need to liaise closely with the family and seek outside support if necessary. Transgender issues also point to the importance of reviewing the SRE curriculum to ensure that there is sufficient work on gender stereotyping and, additionally, considering carefully practices such as lining up boys and girls separately. (For more information visit the Gender Identity Research and Education Society at http://www.gires.org.uk.)

Religious and cultural diversity
In a multicultural and multifaith society, it is important that SRE responds to the range of needs and experiences of all children within the school. This should be based on consultation with the faith communities, not on assumptions about the views of parents/carers. The Sex Education Forum firmly believes that school communities can meet the needs of all children by working together to find common ground and to appropriately value the range of views and faith perspectives on sex and sexuality. It is also important to address misunderstandings about SRE and, in some cases, opposition to SRE. The underlying principles include that:

- Children and young people have an entitlement to SRE that is relevant to them, supports their learning about different faiths and cultures, and is underpinned by values promoting equality and respect and access to accurate and reliable information.
- Valuing diversity and anti-discriminatory practice must be an integral part of the school's ethos, reflected in all areas of the curriculum. In SRE, this involves professionals taking responsibility for having knowledge and understanding about the sensitivities within some faith communities, consulting and involving faith communities in the development of policy and practice.
- We need to create a safe framework in which parents and carers from faith communities, and members of the wider community, understand more about SRE, are able to discuss their views and beliefs, and feel involved in the process of developing SRE.

In multifaith and multicultural schools it is important that the SRE policy also includes, in line with equalities duties, the school's perspective on forced marriage, female genital mutilation (FGM), and family diversity, including same-sex relationships, civil partnerships, divorce, single parenthood and children's rights. For more information see 'Religion and other Beliefs in Sex & Relationships Education' (SEF 2013).

Children with additional learning needs including physical disability
Pupils with additional learning needs have an equal right to appropriate SRE. The SRE programme may benefit from multi-agency preparation, planning and, where appropriate, delivery. The needs of the children, of teaching staff (especially learning support assistants and others working more directly to support teachers), and of parents and carers have to be identified and addressed. The vulnerability of children with learning difficulties makes the provision of SRE that addresses personal safety and issues of consent essential. The activities discussed in Chapter 4 include differentiation and may need to be adapted to ensure inclusion. The learning support assistant may need to prepare for the activities prior to the lesson, and doing a follow-up to ensure understanding is equally important. There are many teaching resources available to accommodate a range of needs, and SEF produces resource lists for primary, secondary and special schools (www.sexeducationforum.org.uk).

Family diversity
Children live within a diverse range of family units: some children will have two parents who are married or cohabiting, others will be looked after by a local authority, live with one parent through separation or bereavement, while others may live with lesbian, gay, bisexual or transgender parents or aunts, uncles or grandparents. Equalities legislation is clear that children must not be discriminated against due to their family background, and the school's perspective on equalities and diversity should be mentioned in its SRE policy.

Understanding this diversity of experience can helpfully be built into all work on relationships to nurture empathy, understanding and pride. A focus on building core values of love, commitment, honesty, trust and respect within relationships helps children to value the richness of different relationships and to develop competence in making, sustaining and, where necessary, ending relationships.

Masturbation
The issue of masturbation may arise, particularly with younger children and children with special needs whereby they are inappropriately touching themselves during lessons. How the school will deal with these issues will need to be included in its SRE policy. All staff in school need to be confident and comfortable with a supportive language when talking to children and their parents/carers about this. Children need to know that it is acceptable to touch themselves, but that it should be done in private, not in public places like school. These messages may have to be repeated often for some children with particular learning difficulties.

How masturbation will be explored in the curriculum will also need to be considered, and teachers will need to ensure they feel confident to discuss this in relation to girls and boys and to answer questions. Lessons about personal boundaries and safe/unsafe touch may provide opportunities for this issue to be raised. Teachers will also want to remind pupils of the different faith perspectives on this issue (see SEF resources on religion and belief).

Domestic violence

Domestic violence can be found in every socio-economic group and community. Crime statistics show that, despite some variation, most perpetrators are male and most victims are female. Nationally, more than one in four women will experience domestic violence in their lifetime after the age of 16; this is equivalent to approximately 4.5 million women (Home Office 2010). It is estimated that 200,000 children in England live in households where there is a known risk of domestic violence (Lord Laming 2009).

Therefore, primary schools through child protection and pastoral support procedures need to be able to identify and potentially support children living in families where there is domestic violence, and a reference to this should be included in the SRE policy. Additionally, schools need to ensure a clear focus on gender stereotyping and healthy and non-violent relationships is at the core of their SRE programme (see the Women's Aid 'Expect Respect' resource at www.womensaid.org.uk).

Equalities, diversity and anti-bullying

Effective SRE develops children's understanding of diversity and difference, and promotes equality and healthy relationships as well as developing children's skills to challenge stereotypes and prejudice. This element of SRE is threaded throughout a good SRE programme and can particularly be found in the themes of 'My body' and 'Relationships'. The SRE policy must be linked to the school's equalities and anti-bullying policy.

3

Good practice in the planning and delivery of SRE

Good practice in the planning, delivery and assessment of SRE

Planning SRE

It is essential that the results of the audit and consultation processes are used to inform the planning of primary school SRE programmes in the short, medium and long term. A programme that meets the needs of the children should be developed, and teachers should feel prepared and confident to create a safe learning environment and be skilled in the methods and resources used to deliver SRE. Teachers also need the skills to deal with unexpected questions, behaviours and issues as they arise.

Preparing teachers for SRE

In many primary schools SRE is delivered by form teachers. Therefore, it is essential that all primary teachers receive training to support them in the effective planning and delivery of SRE. It is good practice for this training to explore the attitudes and values underpinning SRE and to develop teacher skills in creating a safe learning environment and the use of active teaching and learning methods. Teachers particularly appreciate an opportunity to explore how to answer questions and deal with sensitive issues. Regular updates are extremely important.

Some teachers may find teaching SRE particularly difficult or challenging, and will need extra support from the PSHE education coordinator and/or the school nurse. Some male teachers have reported feeling nervous about teaching about menstruation, and some female teachers about wet dreams. Good preparation is useful for building confidence on less familiar topics. The gender of the teacher should not make any difference to effective delivery provided that a safe learning environment is created and the teacher approaches the subject matter confidently. Where possible, single-gender work benefits from being facilitated by an adult of the same gender, but this is not always possible and is not the single most important issue. Pupils will be more concerned about the teacher's approach and willingness to answer questions than their gender.

Organising SRE

Different schools organise their SRE programmes in different ways, and it is important for programmes to reflect the needs of the school community and for there to be clarity about a programme's intended learning outcomes. Other opportunities such as literacy can be used to enrich and reinforce understanding and skills. Possible methods of delivery comprise:

- discrete PSHE education lessons
- learning opportunities on social and emotional aspects of learning (SEAL) in PSHE education, across the curriculum and through small group work
- topics and a creative curriculum focusing on new life/growth, ourselves, keeping healthy and people who help us: for example, if a school keeps laying hens the children can learn about the life cycles

> It was really important that our school had a staff meeting to refresh everyone's thinking around a subject – especially such a sensitive subject as SRE. I loved the session because it enthused me and enabled me to plan teaching this subject differently.
>
> Year 4 teacher

- science (biological knowledge-based aspects)
- religious education (faith perspectives on marriage and civil partnerships)
- literacy (social stories and exploration of emotions and attitudes)
- circle time
- assemblies (anti-bullying, respect, difference and diversity)
- the theme of the week
- playground games
- 'Home' corner
- story sacks.

Groupings for SRE teaching

It is good practice for most SRE to be taught in mixed groups so that boys and girls are encouraged to work with each other and to understand puberty for both genders. However, some primary schools have found it useful to plan their discrete provision so that all classes throughout the school are doing PSHE education at the same time. This provides extended opportunities to organise different groupings depending on the focus of the lesson.

Single-gender groups

Whilst it is important that boys and girls follow the same curriculum, there may be occasions when single-gender groups are appropriate, and certain parents/carers may also find it more culturally acceptable for SRE to be taught separately to boy and girls. Schools sometimes respond to this requirement by organising particular SRE sessions as single-gender groupings, especially for the biological aspects of SRE. Many schools also provide separate sessions for girls on the practical aspects of managing periods in school, alongside a separate session for boys based on their particular needs, such as worries about erections and shaving. Some schools have run a successful plenary-type session with a quiz, where the boys set questions on aspects of boys' development for the girls and vice versa.

Children with gender identity issues and their parents/carers may need to be consulted on which group they would like to attend. The effective use of ground rules should ensure that the rest of the group accept the choice made by a particular child.

Mixed-age groups

For some primary schools, particularly in rural areas, SRE is taught in mixed-age classes using differentiated learning activities. This might be in terms of outcome; 'a task for all' that individuals in the group can achieve at their own level; extension activities to increase understanding; support on the task, such as help with reading out instructions; different resources; or grouping by ability or by mixed ability. Tasks can also be differentiated – for example with younger pupils focusing on the emotional/relationship issues and older pupils focusing on biological aspects as appropriate to their age groups.

Outside visitors

Many schools make good use of outside visitors to supplement their SRE programmes. Visitors might include a parent or carer with their baby, health promotion staff or the school nurse. It is good practice to involve children in the planning of these sessions, to decide what they would like to see covered and to prepare questions for the visitor.

It is important that the school includes reference to the use of visitors in its policies and as a minimum there should be a meeting between the visitor and teacher before the lesson. A code of practice for the use of external agencies might include:

- Clarifying the purpose and role of the outside visitor within the SRE programme.
- Clarifying the boundaries of their input.
- Ensuring outside visitors are aware of the values framework for SRE sessions, the planned curriculum and relevant school policies.
- Highlighting the aims and objectives of any session and identifying the learning outcomes.
- Planning and agreeing how the visitor will work with the teacher, including the importance of the teacher always remaining in the room to support the visitor, and how to ensure that issues raised as a result of the session can be addressed appropriately after the visitor has left.
- Providing a mechanism for pupil, teacher and visitor evaluation of the session to inform future planning.
- Establishing lines of accountability between the outside visitor and the school, and making them explicit.

For more information on this topic see SEF's *External Visitors Factsheet*, available at www.sexeducationforum.org.uk.

Choosing resources

There are a wide range of resources on the market that primary schools can use as part of their SRE curriculum. However, it is important that resources are chosen to specifically support the learning outcomes of the lesson. When selecting resources or activities, check that they are consistent with the aims and objectives of your policy. The following checklist is helpful when choosing resources.

> Activity packs can be useful in generating ideas and suggestions when putting together your programme, but don't be afraid to change and adapt resources to suit the needs of the children in your class.
>
> Primary school teacher

Checklist for choosing resources

☐ Will the resource help the children to achieve the intended learning outcomes of the lesson? Does it add value to the lesson?

☐ Have parents/carers and governors been consulted about the use of the resource? Is it culturally appropriate for the school population?

☐ Has the resource been used before and, if so, what was the feedback from pupils, parents/carers and staff?

☐ Is the resource appropriate in terms of the language and images for the age group, level of maturity and existing knowledge and understanding of the pupils?

☐ Are the information and images factually accurate, up to date, and presented in a balanced and objective way?

☐ Does the resource promote positive images of diversity and an inclusive approach to SRE, or is it biased and encouraging stereotyping?

☐ Can the resource be adapted for all children within the class?

☐ Are there instructions on how to use the resource? Are they clear? Can it be used flexibly?

☐ Does the resource allow you to assess and take into account the children's existing knowledge? If yes, how?

☐ Does the resource allow participation and active learning?

☐ Does it conform to legal requirements for SRE; and is there reference to how it helps users meet statutory and non-statutory learning outcomes, including those of the National Curriculum PSHE Education Framework?

☐ Does the resource include procedures or methods by which learning outcomes can be monitored, assessed and/or evaluated? If so, how do these procedures or methods work?

☐ Is there information on relevant agencies/organisations or other sources of information/support?

☐ Where appropriate, does the resource encourage parental/carer understanding and involvement?

☐ Is there any preparation or research required to use the activity?

☐ Is the resource well designed? Is it durable, easy to use and easy to store?

☐ Is the resource good value for money?

Experienced teachers of SRE tell us that there is no such thing as the definitive SRE resource. They suggest that each school puts together its own series of activities, which can be selected from a range of activity packs. Even the best resources will include activities that need to be amended to suit the needs of a class.

There are many excellent picture books and story books that are now available to support the teaching of SRE. Some of these are a matter of individual taste – some using humour, while others are more medical – but all would need to be examined against the checklist above and school policy. Teachers may also need to work with children to ensure children are clear about which elements are factually correct and which have been embellished or made amusing to make the book readable and fun.

Supporting parents/carers as educators

Many children report that they want their parents/carers to be their main source of information about sex and relationships. For some parents/carers this task comes naturally, but for others it can be a daunting prospect. The school will want to make it clear that it values the role of the parent/carer as their child's principal health educator. Primary schools have found a range of ways to provide practical support for parents/carers to help them in talking with their children about feelings and relationships, and in answering questions about growing up, sex and sexual orientation.

> I don't know what it is like to discuss these things with your parents but I would like to find out.
> Year 6 child

> It's crucial to have parents on board with the teaching because they are a valuable resource in providing back-up for their child's education.
> Year 3 teacher

Case study

'It's alright to talk to Mum and Dad'
One school in Cumbria runs 'Mothers and Daughters' sessions. A letter of invitation is given to all Key Stage 2 girls explaining that if their mother is not available then a grandmother, older sister or other trusted adult can come along. The school also ensures that there are female staff available so no girl is excluded if her mother cannot come.

The theme of the evening is 'growth and change'. Each girl is given a folder to use and take home. Topics covered include: what we need to grow, puberty, female body parts and menstruation. All activities are interactive, such as quizzes, matching text to pictures, and discussion. People can choose to find a space to work within the hall, or can move into adjacent classrooms if they want more space and privacy.

A positive feeling tends to develop during the session, with meaningful interaction between mothers and their daughters. Following positive feedback, the school set up a 'Dads and Lads' event for Key Stage 2 boys.

These sessions provide parents/carers with the opportunity to engage with their children on a subject they might otherwise find difficult to broach, and to send out the message that 'It's alright to talk to Mum and Dad', and as one parent reported, 'The school has started the process rolling for us parents and I think it's a great thing. It's a great tool for parents then to be able to move the subject forward.'

Primary school support for parents/carers can take many forms. For example:

- Provide parents/carers with leaflets about talking to their child about sex (from, for example, fpa, SEF or Parentline) and links to websites with further information and guidance on the subject. The information should be generally available on the school website and parents'/carers' attention can be drawn to it when SRE is being delivered to their child.
- Provide parents/carers with age-appropriate lists of books they can read with their children. Where possible, operate a school system for loaning books to parents or liaise with the local library to find out what they can provide and then advertise these. Alternatively, you could stock books in the school's own library or parent room.
- Include sessions on 'talking to your children about sex and relationships' as part of a general SRE meeting, or as part of a carousel of support meetings for parents.
- Ensure parents/carers are aware of the values underpinning the school SRE programme, and build parental confidence to communicate family values related to SRE to their children and young people. For example, some parents might want their children to wait until they are married before they have sex; some will want to highlight the importance of condom use and pleasure; while others will want to reassure their children that they can ask them anything.
- Homework tasks create opportunities for children and young people to talk to their parents/carers, their relatives and the wider community about SRE. For example, as a research task pupils can ask their parents what kind of SRE they had when they were at school. Pupils can take home worksheets completed during an SRE lesson with a summary of what has been covered and suggestions for follow-up discussion topics at home (and this information could also be given to any parents who choose to withdraw their children from SRE).
- Running short courses for parents and carers to build up knowledge and confidence on talking to their children about sex and relationships – for example the FPA 'Speakeasy' course. For more information, visit www.fpa.org.uk. The design and content of these courses should be informed by the age and needs of the children and their parents/carers.
- Linking with local parenting strategies – for example, building sessions on SRE into parenting courses offered by Sure Start and Children's Centres.

Delivering SRE

Creating a safe environment

Working agreements and ground rules

At the beginning of the SRE programme, the children in the class should develop a working agreement containing ground rules. These rules should be written by the children themselves in language they understand and displayed in a prominent place. Rules should be referred to at the beginning of each lesson and they should be reviewed and revised when necessary. The development of ground rules with the children will help create to a safe environment in which to deliver SRE by:

- Contributing to a feeling of safety and therefore facilitating participation in the lesson.
- Reducing the possibility of disrespectful behaviour and the disclosure of inappropriate personal information by pupils.

- Enabling an environment in which pupils can develop and practise the skills that will help them become more confident speakers, active listeners and more effective, sensitive communicators.
- Reducing teachers' concerns about unexpected questions or comments from pupils.

Example ground rules should be included in the school's SRE policy and shared with parents/carers, but good practice would be to negotiate ground rules with the class. These ground rules will build on, but be different to school rules.

Developing ground rules with younger pupils

A circle time activity can be used to develop ground rules. For example, pupils are asked to name a game they like to play, and then imagine an alien has landed on earth. How would the alien know how to play the game and what rules would apply? Go round the circle naming a rule from the game, and then discuss what it feels like when someone does not follow the rules? What could happen if no one followed the rules? Why are rules helpful? This then leads into ground rules for when the children are learning together in SRE. Makaton and pictures can be used to support written ground rules and ensure they are inclusive to the group.

Developing ground rules with older pupils

Put pupils into groups and give them a Post-it and ask each of them to write down one positive action that would make them feel more comfortable (no names are attached). These rules are then discussed and prioritised in the groups, and the groups identify five rules on a large sheet of paper displayed for everyone to discuss. From the suggestions collected and discussed, hold a vote to identify the most commonly felt needs of the group. The process of eventually arriving at a consensus is valuable in itself, with pupils learning what others think is important.

Once ground rules have been developed it is crucial that these are displayed every lesson and referred back to on a regular basis. Sometimes the ground rules are signed by all members of the group as a contract. Teachers should praise pupils keeping to the ground rules and the whole class should be encouraged to appropriately challenge those who do not. In addition, rewards can be given for keeping to the rules (such as for listening to each other). At the end of a lesson pupils can be asked to agree which rules they kept to and which they did not, or asked if any others need to be added.

An effective set of ground rules will contain the elements shown in the text box – in language that is age appropriate to the class and where possible formulated as positive behaviours. For example, 'We will listen to each other' and 'We will use the agreed language'.

Example of ground rules

We will try:

- to be kind to each other
- to listen to each other
- to respect our rights to share different views
- to take care with information we share about ourselves and other people
- to remember that we can always talk about things in private with an adult in school, but the adult may have to share information if they are worried about our safety
- not to ask personal questions.

Distancing techniques and answering questions

To avoid disclosures, teaching activities should aim to use distancing techniques, such as role play and puppets. The use of a question box also allows children to ask questions anonymously. Schools will also need to explore and agree how they will respond to questions asked in lessons. Staff should try to anticipate which issues might come up in a lesson and consider how they should respond. It is recommended that schools devise a set of responses to questions and use this as a 'script' to build confidence and ensure staff are working in support of the school's values.

The answers to any question should always be age appropriate and will therefore vary in detail and approach. It may help to keep responses simple and specific to what is known of the individual asking the question.

There are lots of ways of answering these questions that will be appropriate to your school and pupils. As a principle, questions should be answered because, if a child could ask their parent/carer, then it is likely they would already have done so. Adults in the classroom can model effectively the importance of being able to talk about sex and relationships, and that there is no shame in asking a question or being concerned about something. Sometimes it may be appropriate to give simple answers to the whole group, but a more in-depth answer one to one, especially if the question is beyond the maturity of the class.

It is very important to stress mutual respect and that in all relationships we should never force anyone to do anything they do not want to do. Also stress it is always acceptable to tell someone if something is happening that feels wrong or inappropriate. Staff must be prepared to follow child protection procedures if a child says anything that worries them.

Suggestions for responding to questions

- If a question is of a personal nature, remind the pupils of the ground rule, 'No one has to answer personal questions'.
- A question does not need to be answered immediately. If the teacher is unsure or needs extra time they can say something

like, 'That's tricky. I'm not sure about that. We'll look into that next time.' The question could go into the question box, or might be being covered in subsequent lessons, but it must be responded to in some way.

- When appropriate, question boxes or 'Ask-it' baskets can be used to collect questions that the teacher can read and then plan an age-appropriate answer. These questions will also help assess learner needs and inform planning for future lessons. The questions should be kept anonymous when responding in public. Another method for responding to the questions might be to type them out and give them to groups of pupils to try to answer.
- Sometimes a pupil may raise an issue that is too advanced for the class. In this case the teacher can defer the question so that it can be answered in a small group or one to one. An individual can also be referred to the school nurse, school counsellor or service if they want further support. If there is cause for concern, the teacher should discuss this in confidence with the school child protection officer to agree next steps.
- There may be something happening in the school community that causes an increase in SRE-related questions – for example, a member of staff is pregnant, or a pupil has a bereavement. It is important to answer the children honestly and in an age-relevant way. It may also be worth informing parents of what is happening and encouraging them also to talk to their children about the issue.
- It is often helpful to respond to a question by first checking out what the pupil already knows, or by asking for further clarification; for example, 'What do you think that word means?' or 'Where have you heard that word used?'
- Colleagues or the PSHE education coordinator can always be consulted for support. It may be appropriate (having agreed with the pupil) to liaise with parents/carers about questions that have been asked and answered.
- Lengthy or complicated responses are not usually necessary; a simple and concrete piece of information offers clarity and may avoid confusion.
- In responding to certain questions, recognise different views are held – for example, about contraception and abortion.
- Place a response to a question within the context of the school's SRE curriculum, past and in the future: 'At the moment we are looking at "X", although in Year 4 you will look at "Y" in more detail'.

Agreeing a language
Using agreed language will be one of the key ground rules for SRE lessons. The words we choose when discussing sex and relationships and how we express ourselves send out strong messages about how we feel about the subject.

To facilitate learning about sex and relationships teachers need to be comfortable with the words they choose and how they say them. Training and practice is essential so that teachers feel confident and are able to use sexual vocabulary when speaking aloud. Adults and pupils in the classroom may occasionally feel embarrassed and the teacher may want to acknowledge this at the beginning of lessons by saying it is alright to be embarrassed, but then focusing on the importance of the learning ahead. Modelling that it is acceptable to talk about sex and relationships is an important message to pupils.

The language used to name external body parts or genitalia can be a particular worry for primary school teachers. Younger children may only recognise familial names for genitalia, which vary widely from family to family. But children also need to learn a shared vocabulary so that they can understand and be understood by children and adults outside their family. Medical terms such as penis, testicles, vulva and vagina provide this shared vocabulary. Learning these terms is essential so that children can seek help if they are being abused or need medical advice, and so that they can learn about their body and be prepared for growing up.

Teachers may wish to plan and write down a list of words that will be introduced in a lesson and over the course of a year, along with agreed definitions. Some schools have found it useful to negotiate and share this vocabulary list with parents/carers. The fact that medical terms will be used to describe genitalia can also be referenced in the school SRE policy. Use of language can be discussed with pupils as part of the ground rules.

The language used in SRE lessons should always be inclusive and affirm diversity. Terms such as partner rather than girlfriend or boyfriend should be used, civil partnership should be acknowledged alongside marriage, and assumptions that all children and young people are or will grow up to be heterosexual should be avoided, or that they have heterosexual parents.

Fostering positive relationships and challenging prejudice
To maintain a positive learning environment teachers need to develop effective skills in challenging prejudice when it occurs. It is likely that some SRE lessons will result in pupils expressing racist, homophobic, sexist or other prejudiced views. How the teacher responds to this prejudice is important. Aggressive or inappropriate challenge can impede learning by alienating individuals and making them feel defensive. Similarly, prejudice that goes unchallenged will also alienate individuals or groups and will reinforce the prejudiced view. Within and outside of lessons, staff need to be confident to challenge prejudice, including the derogatory use of the word 'gay', or expressions like 'don't be such a girl'.

Challenge can be made in different ways. It may be as simple as referring the group back to the working agreement or to school values. A challenge could be offered implicitly by naming the prejudice or using inclusive language. The group could also be asked, 'Why do you think some people think that?' Staff in schools will need to work within their school equalities policies and ensure any incidents are recorded in line with these policies.

Every effort should be made to acknowledge different faith perspectives on issues related to sex and relationships. This affirms the beliefs of children and young people in the class and helps all to understand the range of views in society. Nevertheless, it is important that teachers are aware of the school's ethos on equalities and diversity issues, especially with regard to same-sex relationships, civil partnerships, single parenthood, divorce, forced marriage, masturbation and female genital mutilation.

Dealing with personal disclosures

There may be occasions when a pupil discloses a personal issue either in a lesson or afterwards. It is important to reach agreement with the class about confidentiality before personal disclosures are made. Teachers should explain that the classroom is a public place and not somewhere to discuss very personal issues. They should, however, ensure that the children know who they can talk to on a one-to-one basis if they want to discuss any concerns or worries. Teachers and other staff cannot however guarantee complete confidentiality. If the child is at risk of harm they must follow the school's safeguarding/child protection procedures.

If a child does becomes distressed within a lesson, it may be appropriate for the learning support assistant to take them out of the classroom and contact the head of pastoral care.

Children who have been sexually abused may find SRE lessons particularly difficult and, where schools know of a child's past experience, they should talk with the child and their parent/carer about their attendance in lessons and perhaps provide them with a right to pass or leave the lesson when and if it is difficult. However, if a child is removed from SRE lessons every attempt should be made to provide them with a parallel programme, perhaps delivered by the school nurse or someone with a therapy background.

Similarly, schools may occasionally find that they have children who are displaying sexually inappropriate and even sexually aggressive behaviours. A social services referral may be required in these circumstances and referral to a specialist. This child will need to be supported while also keeping the rest of the school community safe.

Active learning methods

Teachers report that programmes involving active, participatory learning methods used in the context of a group are the most effective at engaging pupils. Active learning methods work well and provide the most valuable learning experiences for children, particularly those for whom English is not their first language, those with low literacy levels and those who may be reluctant to take part in lessons.

The methods can be fun and actively engage children in their own learning process by enabling them to draw on their own experience. They support the development of core life skills – an integral part of good quality SRE. By working collaboratively, children are encouraged to use communication skills and decision-making skills, and to learn how to articulate an idea and share that idea with others.

Active learning uses creative processes to develop skills, and pupils work through a sequence of principles in order to learn. As illustrated in the accompanying diagram, this involves 'doing' or engaging in a structured activity – for example, a problem-solving exercise – and sharing the experience by reflecting on the activity and describing it in process terms. What has been learnt is practised and is followed by planning future behaviour, by working out what has been learnt and how that will change behaviour in the future.

The learning cycle

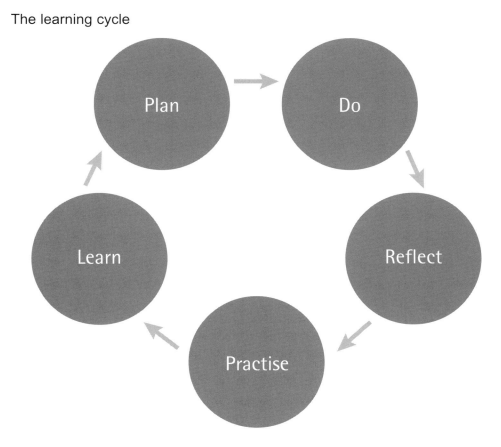

Active learning methods can be fun and effective, but equally if not well planned and practised beforehand can feel threatening and awkward to both teacher and student. It can seem as if you are relinquishing control of the class, but in fact you are sharing control with the group and you are still responsible for the learning, discipline and safe environment.

Examples of active learning methods: Opening activities

- **Mind maps** – a technique sometimes referred to as brainstorming or 'thought showers', which involves children being asked to provide words they think of in response to a subject given by the teacher. The teacher then facilitates discussion around the words provided. Asking, for example, 'Are they positive or negative words?' and 'What would it feel like to have these words directed at you?'
- **Circle activities** – a useful technique to facilitate a safe and positive environment for children to take turns (if they want to) talking about a specific issue, such as feelings and relationships. For more information visit http://www.circle-time.co.uk.

Examples of active learning methods: Talking and listening activities

- **Discussion** – an activity where children, working in small groups, are given a question to answer before giving feedback on their discussion to the whole group. Alternatively, children work in pairs then give feedback in groups of four.
- **Listening exercises** – where children work in pairs, with one of them listening carefully while the other speaks. They then swap roles. They

can then give feedback on what they have learnt to a small group or the whole class.

Examples of active learning methods: Exploring attitudes and beliefs

- **Continuums** – a way for children to hear and understand a range of views. A statement is read out by a teacher and the children are then asked to physically place themselves along a line that best reflects their opinion or view on it (acceptable or not acceptable; agree or disagree). The teacher then facilitates discussion based on the positions taken.
- **Card sort** – a good activity for consensus building. Pupils are either asked to write a statement on a piece of card or are given ready-made cards. In turn, each pupil picks a card and reads out the statement. After all the cards have been picked the pupils need to come to an agreement on how to organise them (for example, whether they can agree or disagree with the statements).

Examples of active learning methods: Distancing techniques

- **Case studies or scenarios** – where children have the opportunity to consider the consequences of the actions of characters in a case study, and to reflect on how things could have been done differently.
- **Storytelling** – a way of using fiction to explore feelings and attitudes, with the group being asked, for example, how they would resolve the issues raised. Children can be asked to develop their own stories too. (For examples of suitable children's literature see the Primary School Resources lists at www.sexeducationforum.org.uk.)
- **Puppets** – an effective resource, either home-made or commercially produced, that some schools have used with children to explore issues such as friendships, bullying and HIV/AIDS.
- **Role play and drama** – a way of allowing children to explore feelings and ideas in a practical, real-life situation. It may be done in pairs, small or large groups, and be teacher- or child-led. To be effective, careful management is vital, with debriefing and processing to draw out the learning.

Examples of active learning methods: Group activities

- **Collages/posters/drawings** – illustrating a theme or topic in a way that children enjoy. Collages could focus on 'What's a family?' or 'Babies', but could also include images relating to gender stereotypes. Posters could be designed by children to advertise people and agencies that can help children. Drawings could be made showing the outline of a child with labels to mark the names of body parts.
- **ICT** – an effective resource for encouraging active participation: for example, using a large-scale picture, mind map or timeline on an interactive whiteboard. Membership of a regional broadband consortium or grid for learning will provide access to a wide range of recommended ICT resources such as pictures.
- **Timelines** – a useful way of looking at human development. Children mark on a line those things they could do at different stages of their lives; or they help a teacher fill in what they know about a baby's development, starting two days after its birth and working backwards along the timeline. Older children may like to mark the significant times

in their lives – for example, the birth of a sibling, a change of school, a friend moving away, or a relative or pet dying.

Examples of active learning methods: Reflections

- **Rounds** – an integral part of circle or any active group work. Rounds are often used at the end of a session as a way of getting everyone to sit together and briefly share ideas and feelings. Children are invited to complete a sentence – for example, 'One thing I learned/enjoyed today was …'
- **Individual reflection** – can take place in the context of a diary. Questions asked could include, 'How do I feel?', 'What have I learnt in this lesson', 'What have I learnt about myself?' and 'What did I learn about others in the group?'

Assessment of SRE

Assessment is as important in PSHE education as in every other curriculum area and for the same reasons: children and young people have a right to know how they are doing in every subject; teachers need to know how pupils are progressing, in order to inform future teaching and learning; the school leadership team, parents, governors and, of course, Ofsted inspectors need to see the impact PSHE education is having for young people and the part it is playing for the school in achieving the three statutory aims of the National Curriculum … [and meeting] higher grade descriptors of the … Ofsted framework. If we do not assess learning, then all we can do is describe what we do in PSHE education but not what impact it has.

(PSHE Association 2011)

Assessment plays a key role in effective SRE teaching and learning. Assessment is a process through which judgements are made about an individual's learning and development. It is not about making judgements on the character, worth or values of individual pupils, nor is it about continual testing. Assessment should also not be confused with evaluation. Assessment, in SRE as in any subject, is an integral part of learning. Teachers should not rely entirely on pupil self-assessment, which should be supported by evidence of achievement. Although there is no attainment target for PSHE education, end of Key Stage Statements for PSHE were developed by QCDA (see www.teacherfind.com) to help teachers assess progress. These statements, summarised in the accompanying text box, are useful for planning PSHE education programmes.

End of Key Stage statements for PSHE education

These statements describe the types and range of performance that the majority of pupils should characteristically demonstrate by the end of the Key Stage, having been taught a relevant programme of PSHE. The statements are designed to help teachers judge levels of achievement and the extent to which their pupils are making progress.

Key Stage 1

Children can identify and name some feelings (for example through interpreting facial expressions) and express some of their positive qualities. They are able to demonstrate that they can manage some feelings in a positive and effective way. They begin to share their views and opinions (for example, talking about fairness), and they can set themselves simple goals (for example, sharing toys).

Children can make simple choices about some aspects of their health and well-being (for example, by choosing between different foods and between physical activities, knowing that they need sun protection) and understand what keeps them healthy (for example, exercise and rest). They can explain ways of keeping clean (for instance by washing their hands and keeping their hair tidy) and they can name the main parts of the body. Children can talk about the harmful aspects of some household products and medicines, and describe ways of keeping safe in familiar situations (for example, knowing how and where to cross the road safely). They can explain that people grow from young to old.

Children can recognise that bullying is wrong and can list some ways to get help in dealing with it. They can recognise the effect of their behaviour on other people, and can cooperate with others (for example, by playing and working with friends or classmates). They can identify and respect differences and similarities between people, and can explain different ways that family and friends should care for one another (for instance, telling a friend that they like them or showing concern for a family member who is unwell).

Key Stage 2

Children can demonstrate that they recognise their own worth and that of others (for example, by making positive comments about themselves and classmates). They can express their views confidently and listen to and show respect for the views of others. They can identify positive ways to face new challenges (for example, the transition to secondary school). They can discuss some of the bodily and emotional changes that take place at puberty, and can demonstrate some ways of dealing with these in a positive way. They can talk about a range of jobs, and explain how they will develop skills to work in the future. They can also demonstrate how to look after and save money.

Children can make choices about how to develop healthy lifestyles (for instance, by knowing the importance of a healthy diet and regular exercise). They can identify some factors that affect emotional health and well-being (like exercise or dealing with emotions). They can make judgements and decisions and can list some ways of resisting negative peer pressure around issues affecting their health and well-being. They can list the commonly available substances and drugs that are legal and illegal, and can describe some of the effects and risks of these. They can also identify and explain how to manage the risks in different familiar situations (for example, discussing issues connected to personal safety).

Children can explain how their actions have consequences for themselves and others. They can describe the nature and consequences of bullying, and can express ways of responding to it. They can identify different types of relationship (for example, marriage or friendships), and can show ways to maintain good relationships (by, for instance, listening, supporting and caring). They can respond to, or challenge, negative behaviours such as stereotyping and aggression. They can also describe some of the different beliefs and values in society, and can demonstrate respect and tolerance towards people different from themselves.

There are a number of different types of assessment that are carried out, each with a different purpose in mind. Assessment is used to assess both what has been learnt and what needs to be learnt. The key types of assessment (as described in the following subsections) are:

- baseline (assessment for learning)(or needs assessment)
- formative (assessment for learning)
- summative (assessment of learning).

Teachers will need to be clear about what it is they are assessing and will need to use levels or end of Key Stage statements against which they can assess progress.

Reflection is the basis of all assessment and links to formative assessment (discussed below). It is important to allow enough time at the end of the session for pupils to reflect on what they have achieved and experienced by taking part in the activity, otherwise the group can go away having enjoyed the activity but not knowing what the point of the exercise was. This information can also be used to assess what has been learnt and understood and to inform the planning of future lessons. Some typical questions are:

- What was it like doing this activity today?
- How are you feeling?
- What did you learn by listening to people's opinions that were different from your own?
- What skills did you learn and practise today?
- Do you think your learning today will change or influence your behaviour?

Baseline assessment

Baseline or needs assessment (assessment for learning) is carried out at the beginning of a piece of work for three specific purposes:

- to determine what is already known
- to clarify learning needs
- to identify whether children or young people have any special educational needs (if not already known).

Practitioners carry out a baseline assessment to determine where to start, and to guide them in how the work should be developed, including what language and resources to use. Needs assessment is particularly important in SRE because different groups of children of the same age will have different needs related to this subject. For parents/carers it is reassuring to know that planning has been in response to children's existing knowledge and the questions they have. Here are some methods that can be used to assess needs and inform planning.

Question box

The anonymous questions asked by pupils may well inform the need to make changes to an existing programme. For example, contraception is generally not taught in much detail in primary schools; however, if a number of questions are being asked about it a teacher may respond by planning a very simple, age-appropriate lesson on contraception.

Draw and write

Working individually, children can for example be asked to draw a child getting up in the morning and preparing for school, writing words around their pictures to explain what they are doing. This could be used to inform lessons on personal hygiene, with gaps in knowledge being addressed through subsequent lesson planning. If knowledge and understanding are already good then the lesson time could be used for a different focus.

Brainstorms and graffiti sheets

Children can be asked individually or in groups to write down or draw everything they already know about a subject and what more they would like to find out. This might be particularly useful when a topic like puberty is being taught for the second time in a programme. If children remember well the physical changes that they were taught in Year 4, then Year 6 lessons can be used, for example, to focus on managing puberty and emotional changes. (See the accompanying text box discussing a draw and write activity.)

Attitude continuums

These can be used to explore and identify any stereotypical attitudes that children might hold related to gender for example, and the results used to plan activities that explore and challenge stereotypes.

Baseline – needs assessment – assessment for learning: Brainstorm

Body changes

Children's drawings are useful for baseline assessment as they can be used with younger children, although they also work well with older children, particularly more vulnerable young people. An example of a draw and write activity is detailed here related to puberty.

The activity focuses on assessing knowledge of the emotional and physical changes that take place during puberty, and could take place as a baseline assessment prior to a unit on puberty. For example, a Year 6 SRE teacher may want to assess how much pupils have remembered from previous years or learnt from home. The drawings could be analysed prior to the next lesson and used to inform planning. For example, if the drawings show that knowledge is good, then teaching in Year 6 could focus on issues involved in managing puberty such as coping with wet dreams, spots or periods. If knowledge is patchy, or better for girls' changes than for boys' changes, then lesson planning can be amended accordingly.

Time

20–40 minutes

Equipment

- Copies of body outline or large paper for children/young people to draw round one of their peers
- Paper
- Felt pens or pencils.

Method

1. For a baseline assessment of the group's needs, children could work in small groups. Working in gender groups may provide interesting information on different knowledge levels of boys and girls.
2. Ask participants to draw a picture of a body, draw round a group member or give out copies of the body outline.
3. Ask them to draw and label the different emotional and physical changes that take place during puberty.
4. If the group are finding this difficult then ask them to think about:
   - heart, mind and feelings
   - skin and hair
   - sex organs
   - voice
   - good things about growing up
   - bad things about growing up.
5. Take away the pictures to help plan lessons that will address any misunderstandings or gaps in knowledge and understanding. Return to these at the end of the unit – can the children add to and make changes to their drawings as a result of the input?
6. Make a display to show the work that pupils have been doing.

Other topics could include, for example, asking the children and young people to draw what they understand about what is meant by family, keeping safe or keeping clean.

Formative assessment

Formative assessment (assessment for learning) occurs when teachers and children work together to make judgements about progress being made against agreed learning objectives. The results are then used to identify the next teaching/learning steps. It is a dynamic, collaborative process that enhances the learning experience. An ongoing process of assessment occurs, with everyone considering, either individually or in a group, the impact on themselves of the learning. See accompanying text box for an example of formative assessment.

Example of a formative assessment activity

Sentence stems

This activity provides feedback on what children have learnt and is a useful way of finding out what else they need to learn. It also provides an opportunity to acknowledge the successes and achievements of the group.

Time

Approximately one minute per person, and the overall time will be dependent on the size of the group. It is important that the activity does not feel rushed and the group has the skills to listen to all group members.

Method

1. Bring everyone together in a circle.
2. Choose a suitable sentence stem (see the example sentence stems below).
3. Invite someone to start and then, from the starter's left side, carry on around the circle. Each person should be encouraged to contribute.
4. Participants have the option to 'Pass' if they wish, but once the round has been completed, offer another chance to contribute.

Example sentence stems

- What I have learnt from today is …
- I have learnt to do …
- What I need to do next is …
- I now understand …
- Something I will change after today is …

These sentences can also be combined. For example: 'What I found out about was … and what I shall do next is …'

Summative assessment

Summative assessment, or assessment of learning, is carried out at the end of a period of time or a piece of work. Progress and achievement is judged in relation to a set of criteria. These criteria or outcomes can be related to, for example, the end of Key Stage statements (see page 42).

The results of the assessment are used to provide quantitative evidence for reporting to parents/carers, teachers and other professionals and for celebrating achievement with pupils. Summative assessment can also be used to develop future learning goals. (See the accompanying text box for an example of summative assessment.)

Example of a summative assessment activity

Advising others
This activity is a useful way of assessing learning on a particular theme by encouraging children to advise someone else.

Time
20 minutes

Equipment
Paper and pens

Method
1. Scenarios could be given to individuals, pairs or small groups. Children needing support could be given word banks or sentence stems to help them complete the task.
2. Devise a scenario, which will assess pupil knowledge of a particular issue, their skills in knowing how to give or deliver advice, or their ability to explore attitudes and values. Ensure that the learning outcome for the activity identifies the skills being assessed. These learning outcomes could be differentiated (that is, all, most or some). Explore with the pupils what the success criteria will be so that they are fully aware of what they need to do to achieve in the task.
3. The children can record their work either as a letter, email, text or, if they are reporting a conversation for example, using speech bubbles.
4. These can be self-, peer- or teacher-assessed and then kept in the personal portfolio or evidence of learning.

Example scenarios
- You are an agony aunt on a teen magazine. Sarah writes to you saying she is 10 and is very worried about her period starting. What advice do you give her?
- Your friend Ahmed is smaller than most other boys in your year. This is making him feel miserable, particularly because he is being teased and called names by a group of girls. What do you do to help him?
- A group of parents and carers who run a helpline have asked you to advise them on how they should talk to young people about puberty and growing up. Write a 'Top Tips' information sheet for them.
- You are a peer mediator. You are told by a girl in Year 5 that she is being harassed by a group of boys in Year 6. What advice do you give her?

Example assessment criteria for the Ahmed scenario
Your friend Ahmed is smaller than most other boys in your year. This is making him feel miserable, particularly because he is being teased and called names by a group of girls. What do you do to help him?

Learning objective
To be able to describe what bullying and stereotyping is and express ways of responding to it (PSHE education end of Key Stage 2 statement).

Intended learning outcomes
- *Working towards:* I can describe what bullying is in simple terms and I can think of one way I could support someone who is being bullied.
- *Working at:* I can explain what bullying and stereotyping are and can think of two ways of supporting someone who is being bullied.
- *Working beyond:* I can explain what bullying and gender stereotyping are and can provide a range of ideas for how someone being bullied can be supported.

Evaluation of SRE

Evaluation is a process through which judgements are made about how effectively particular teaching approaches, activities and materials meet specific learning objectives. Regular evaluation of the SRE programme by the children, parents/carers and teachers involved is vital, and it should form part of an ongoing process. Evaluation of methods enables teachers to plan future work more constructively. Areas to evaluate include:

- Were the children engaged?
- Did we achieve the learning outcome?
- Did girls and boys engage equally with the activity?

Pupils can be involved in evaluating the programme through the use of a variety of methods, such as:

- end rounds
- thumbs up/down
- anonymous written comments, on Post-its for example
- pupil questionnaires
- pupil focus groups.

For a comprehensive guide to assessment and evaluation see the Sex Education Forum publication 'Assessment, Evaluation and Sex & Relationship Education' (Blake and Muttock 2012).

Lesson plans

4

Lesson plans

How to use the lesson plans

The sample lesson plans provide ideas and model different types of participatory methods. They can and should be adapted to the needs of pupils and to ensure that they are in-line with the school's SRE policy. The lesson plans reflect established good practice by integrating the biological elements in the National Curriculum Science and the emotional and social elements of SRE within the PSHE education framework.

These lessons can be taught in any order, and teachers can mix and match activities from different themes, add their own ideas, enrich with activities from other resources and omit things they do not like. Teachers may find that the lesson plans will work better broken down into two or more lessons.

Each lesson plan provides a broad overview and some narrower example learning outcomes. The learning outcomes chosen by the teacher when planning the lesson will be dependent on lesson emphasis and on the age and understanding of the pupils. Good practice would be to negotiate success criteria with pupils for at least some of the activities.

The lesson plans are organised into six broad themes that provide the basis of a comprehensive SRE programme:

1. My body
2. Life cycles
3. Relationships
4. Feelings and attitudes
5. Keeping safe and looking after myself
6. People who can help me.

Organising SRE into themes supports the SRE curriculum planning process. Each theme includes a rationale for why it is important to explore this theme, a range of questions to explore, lesson plan ideas related to the theme and sample assessment activities.

Some assessment activities are suggested at the end of each theme, but again, how learning is assessed will depend on school policy and practice. Best practice would be for PSHE education to be assessed in a similar way to other subjects. Pupils should be aware of the progress they are making in PSHE and what they need to do to improve.

Lesson plans introduce a variety of activities that can be adapted to different topics but give the SRE teacher a basic repertoire from which to build their lessons. Activities should be selected to meet lesson outcomes.

Many of the activities included have been adapted from tried and tested methods used by SRE and PSHE teachers for many years, and versions of a number of them can be found in current SRE/PSHE manuals, SEF publications, SEAL materials and so forth. We would like to acknowledge the huge contribution made to good practice in SRE by all the teachers, trainers and writers who have developed and shared these ideas over time.

Lesson plan breakdown
Key lesson elements comprise:

- **Opening activities** – designed to involve the whole class in an active way and enable each child to participate.
- **Main activity** – also participatory, designed to enable children to achieve the main learning outcomes.
- **Reflection/plenary** – important time to allow children to think over the lesson, make connections and identify what they have learnt. Useful questions include, 'What did we do?', 'How do I feel?', 'What have I learnt?' and 'How can I use this next time?'

Warm-up games can be used to start the lesson, grab the children's attention and engage them all in learning.

Focus on SRE skills
The following skills are introduced and practised in specific lessons:

- listening
- 'I' statements
- assertiveness/saying no
- assessing risks
- empathy/putting oneself in another person's shoes.

Range of questions to explore
Each theme includes a range of questions organised by age to help parents/carers, schools and other educators understand what children want to learn about in relation to growing up, relationships and sex. Some but not all of the questions are explored in the sample lesson plans. It is also recommended that pupils are consulted to ensure the curriculum meets their particular needs. Pupils can help to prioritise which questions they want to explore in curriculum time. Prioritising will help if there is insufficient time to cover everything.

The following table is a summary of the lesson plans and activities set out in this chapter. It serves as a quick reference and an aid to planning. The table outlines the six themes , the titles of the lesson and the range of activities within that lesson. The lessons are also divided into Key Stage 1 and 2.

Lesson plans – a summary

Theme	Title of Lesson & Activities Key Stage 1	Title of Lesson & Activities Key Stage 2
1. My body	*Male and female* **(p58)** Hand to hand/Body outline – labels *Growing and changing* **(p60)** Round/Picture timeline	*Male and female* **(p62)** Ping-pong/Language/Model-making *Growing and changing (Year 3–4)* **(p64)** Timeline/male & female pictures *Puberty (Year 5–6)* **(p66)** Mix 'n' match/Card sort/Lucky dip
2. Life cycles	*Caring for babies and children* **(p71)** Pass the baby/Baby object carousel	*Caring for babies and children* **(p73)** Human bingo/Meet the visitor *Life cycles and reproduction (Year 3–4)* **(p76)** Jigsaws/Match the baby to the carer *Reproduction and birth (Year 5–6)* **(p78)** Picture groups/AVA + quiz etc.
3. Relationships	*Similarities and differences* **(p84)** All change/Portraits *Gender stereotypes* **(p86)** Baby pictures/Toy picture sort *Caring* **(p88)** Car wash/Pet pictures *Friends* **(p90)** A space on my right/Listening pairs *Families of all kinds* **(p92)** Hoops/Family pictures	*Similarities and differences* **(p94)** Pairs and fours/Values continuum *Gender roles and stereotyping* **(p97)** Pass the alien/Gender timeline *Trust and empathy* **(p99)** Trust trains/Extended role play *What is a friend?* **(p102)** Double circles/Friendship circles *Friendship problems* **(p104)** Four corners/'I' statements
4. Feelings and attitudes	*Feelings* **(p110)** Silent rattle/Soft toy *Managing our feelings* **(p112)** How are you?/Puppets A and B	*Identifying and expressing feelings* **(p114)** Pass the mask/Frozen images *What influences my choices?* **(p116)** Choices timeline/Shifting subgroups/Influences spider diagram

Theme	Title of Lesson & Activities Key Stage 1	Title of Lesson & Activities Key Stage 2
5. Keeping safe and looking after myself	*Keeping safe* (p121) Story/Body outline – warning signs *Setting personal boundaries* (p123) Brainstorm/ Body outlines – touches *Keeping yourself clean and healthy* (p125) This is my ear/Kim's game/Mime	*Keeping safe/understanding risk* (p127) All change/Risk continuum card sort *Asserting personal boundaries* (p129) Saying No/Assertiveness trios *Keeping clean and healthy during puberty* (p131) Kim's game/Body outlines – infection
6. People who can help me	*Someone to talk to* (p136) Trust game/Puppet circle activity/ Helping hands	*Someone to talk to* (p138) Listening pairs/Double circles

Theme 1: My body

Introduction

Teachers need a working understanding of simple human biology and the relevant scientific language in order to teach this theme (and also Theme 2: Life cycles) effectively. A good guide to the level of information required is provided in the leaflets, official websites and materials designed for primary age pupils. Those designed for secondary age pupils can also be used by teachers to reinforce their own understanding of human reproduction.

Body parts

Early and accurate naming of children's body parts is vital. Adult inhibitions about scientific vocabulary may cause children to become confused about their bodies. Not knowing the words for parts of your body has serious implications for child protection and, in later years, conversations with the doctor and future partners. This is equally important for both boys and girls.

If children are to develop a positive sense of their bodies, sexual as well as reproductive body parts should be part of their vocabulary. Female body parts such as the clitoris, vagina and vulva are often not talked about in SRE, which could be due to teachers' and parents' anxieties. This absence can deprive girls of a comfortable language about themselves.

Using accurate terminology consistently can also help staff feel more comfortable and confident in teaching about bodies. So as not to embarrass children or undermine teaching at home, it is important to acknowledge that there are lots of other words that are used, while emphasising what the correct words are and that they will be used within the school.

Variation/similarities and differences

The fact that we are all the same in some ways yet different in others is a key piece of learning for children from the earliest years. Children can so easily pick up from the world around them (sometimes at a very early age) prejudiced attitudes based on lack of respect for people who are different from themselves. Such attitudes are at the root of sexism, homophobia and bullying. Primary schools can provide a role model for children by celebrating similarities, differences and teaching children the importance of being individuals. One way of doing this is to explore the similarities and differences between boys and girls and the gender stereotypes that persist in our society.

Beginning to learn about gender equality and to challenge gender stereotypes is an important part of learning what it is to be a male or female in today's society, and it underpins choices children will make about relationships and sexuality as they grow up. In addition, this work will contribute to the prevention of sexist, sexual, homophobic and transphobic

> Sex education is very important because at that stage of your life [puberty] it is like very exciting – but also you get very frightened, and if you don't know …
> Year 5 girl

bullying by developing children's understanding that there are many different ways to be a boy or a girl and to begin to explore the fact that some people do not always identify with either gender or their birth gender.

The issues involved go far beyond the taught curriculum and must be addressed through the ethos and values of the school as a whole. Adults who work with children should be encouraged not to use gender stereotypes in their conversations with children – that is, to no longer say, for example, 'Boys don't cry', 'I want a big strong boy to help me lift the equipment' or 'Girls can't play football'. Make sure that you check through school and class libraries for books that encourage gender stereotyping and focus instead on books that present positive images of girls, boys, men and women in non-stereotypical roles. Find pictures of men and women doing non-stereotypical jobs and display these around the school. Encourage and comment on boys and girls who act outside the usual stereotypes. Make clear to parents through the school brochure and at parents' meetings that the school encourages boys and girls to take part in all activities equally.

Preparing for puberty

All children need to be aware of, and have the skills to manage, both the physical and emotional changes relating to puberty (DfEE 2000). Many children grow up without any formal education about their bodies and the changes that take place. They may also grow up without learning skills such as asking for help or without thinking about gender roles, expectations and relationships. Both boys and girls have told us that they had anxieties and worries about their bodies. It is clear that primary schools have a key role in this, and in supporting the children as these changes occur. Research shows that children cannot always rely on their parents, who may not expect puberty to begin so early or might assume that it will be covered in school sessions. Many schools begin teaching about puberty in Years 3 and 4, following this up in more detail in Years 5 and 6. Teaching puberty at primary school is particularly important if there is evidence that children are entering puberty at an earlier age.

Teaching needs to include reassurance for both boys and girls that it is normal for the onset of puberty to vary widely, and it should include the preparation of early starters. Children also want an opportunity to discuss the emotional side of puberty. As one boy said, 'My sister's so moody now it's impossible to like her!' It is important to prepare children for the likely mood swings, feelings of confusion, embarrassment and shyness they may experience during puberty, without making it all sound gloomy and awful! How we do this carries significant messages both about how we value girls and boys and about their transition into adulthood.

Key questions on 'My body'

Years 1 and 2
- Why are girls' and boys' bodies different?
- What do we call the different parts of girls' and boys' bodies?

Years 3 and 4
- How has my body changed since I was a baby?
- Why is my body changing?
- Why are some children growing quicker than others?
- Why are some girls in my class taller than the boys?
- How do girls and boys grow differently?
- Why are we all different? Is it alright to be different?
- What are similarities and differences between boys and girls?
- Should boys and girls behave differently?

Years 5 and 6
- What is puberty?
- Does everyone go through it? At what age?
- What body changes do boys and girls go through at puberty?
- Why are some girls 'tomboys' and some boys a bit 'girly'?
- Is my body normal? What is a 'normal' body?
- How will my body change as I get older?

Brief summary of changes at puberty

Boys and girls
Remind children that all children, boys or girls, reach puberty at different ages and that this is perfectly normal. Puberty is the body preparing to be able to reproduce and create a new baby. Not only will they experience physical changes but they may also experience new feelings and emotions. All these change can be scary or overwhelming but they are perfectly normal.

Boys and girls will both grow taller and gain weight. Boys and girls grow hair under their arms and around their genitals. Boys and girls sweat more. Some boys and some girls get spots on their faces, chests and backs. Boys and girls may begin to feel emotional and moody or feel very 'giggly' and excitable.

Boys
Voices become deeper. Hair begins to grow on their upper lip and chin. Testicles start to make sperm. Boys may have erections and 'wet dreams'. They may start having feelings of attraction towards other people.

Girls
Hips grow wider and their breasts start to grow larger. Ovaries start to produce eggs (ova). Menstruation begins. They may start having feelings of attraction towards other people.

Menstruation
When a girl reaches puberty, her ovaries will produce an egg (ovum) every month. The egg travels from the ovary along the fallopian tube towards the womb. During her life a woman will produce 400–500 eggs most of which will not be fertilised and will pass out of the body. Every month the womb prepares to receive a fertilised egg by making a thick, soft, spongy lining. If the egg arrives in the womb unfertilised, the egg and the lining of the womb will pass out through the vagina. It looks like thick blood and is called a period. To soak up the womb lining as it passes out through the vagina, girls and women use either an absorbent towel, which is worn in their pants, or a tampon that is inserted into the vagina. Periods will happen every month until the woman is about 50, unless an egg is fertilised by a sperm from a man. When a girl starts her periods, it means that she could get pregnant. On average, the amount of blood leaving the body is about half a small cupful or two tablespoonfuls.

Male and female (Key Stage 1)

By the end of this lesson the children will be able to name the main external parts of the body, understand the differences between male and female, and learn the biological names of the sexual parts as well as understand that all babies, human and animal, have mothers and fathers.

Learning outcomes
- I know the difference between a boy and a girl and can label boys' and girls' body parts.
- I can tell you my family words for boys' and girls' parts and what the scientific name is for this part of the body.

Working agreement
Remind the children of the working agreement and emphasise that it is acceptable to laugh at something funny but not at another person.

Resources needed
- Body outline
- Labels with the correct names of body parts
- Pictures of babies
- Interactive whiteboard (if available).

Opening activity: Hand to hand
Explain to the children that in this activity you will ask them to move around the classroom. Then you will clap your hands and call a number and the name of a part of the body (arms, legs, knees, fingers). At this, the children should join together in groups of the appropriate number with that part of their bodies touching. Repeat with a different number and part of the body.

Main activity: Body outline
In small groups, have a large sheet of paper with a body outline drawn on it (alternatively draw round a child). Ask the children to stick the prepared labels on appropriate parts of the body. Ask them if they know the names of any parts of the body that are inside (lungs, heart, stomach) and draw and label these. Alternatively you could use an interactive whiteboard for this activity, moving and placing labels for naming body parts in response to the children's suggestions.

Now show the children pictures of some babies with few or no clothes on. Talk to the children about what they think each baby is like and what they will be like as they grow up. Ask how we can tell whether each is a boy or a girl? Introduce words like penis, testicles, vulva, vagina and womb and explain that these are the parts that will mean that we can become a mother or a father when we grow up.

Show some pictures of animal babies and their adult parents, then match them into families while talking about the differences between male and female. Include a human trio. Explain that to make a baby you usually need a male and female; a mum and a dad.

Reflection/plenary
- Go round the class, asking each child in turn to complete the sentence 'Something I've learnt about bodies today is …'
- Sing a song about body parts such as *Head and Shoulders, Knees and Toes* or *Dem Bones*.

Differentiation
- *Children needing more of a challenge* – could label the different organs in the body with their name and function: for example 'lungs – help you breathe', 'heart – pumps the blood'.
- *Children with additional learning needs* – could match shapes and words pictorially. Give a line-drawing outline of a body on A3 paper, with outlines of major organs drawn in. Have words on cards that are the same shape as the organ. This reinforces knowledge of where these organs are in the body as well as encouraging word recognition.

What if …
- *Children get very giggly about names of sexual body parts or say that it's dirty to talk about them?* Remind them that people do often giggle if they are talking about something they don't usually talk about, but that it's really important to learn how your body works. Explain that all the parts of the body have an important job to do and that, though we generally keep them private, there's nothing bad about them.
- *A child asks where a baby comes from?* Usually a simple explanation to this question will suffice. For example 'a baby is made by a man and a woman and lives in a woman's womb' (explain that this is why, during pregnancy, women have a big belly). After nine months the baby is born.
- *Follow-up questions?* Children may ask follow-up questions and, depending on the maturity of the class and the school's SRE policy, providing more detail or reading a book on how babies are made and born may be appropriate. If an individual child is asking lots of detailed questions, discuss with their parent/carer if they would like to answer these questions or if they would like you to.

Growing and changing (Key Stage 1)

By the end of this lesson pupils have thought about how they have grown and changed and how they will grow and change in the future.

Learning outcomes
- I can name some of the changes that have happened to me since I was a baby.
- I can name some of that ways in which I will change as I grow up.

Working agreement
Remind the children about the working agreement and emphasise the rules about treating each other with respect and avoiding sharing personal information or asking personal questions. Remind them of who they can talk with (school staff, parents/carers, school nurse) if they have questions. Remind pupils of how the question box works and the limits of school staff confidentiality.

Resources needed
- Diagrams or pictures from a published scheme, magazines or the internet.
- Paper for a timeline.
- Optional – children's own baby photos; baby/toddler photos of staff.

Opening activity: Round
In a circle, the pupils take turns to share one thing they can do now that they could not do before they started school. The teacher can model a response to start the round. Encourage the pupils to come up with new ideas rather than repeating what other children have said. If they get stuck they can pass.

Main activity: Picture timeline
Give each pupil a picture (from a magazine or resource) of a person engaged in a physical activity. Include pictures of people of different genders and ages, from babyhood to adulthood. Fix a large sheet of paper to the wall and ask each pupil in turn to stick their picture along the timeline according to the age when people might be able to do these things. Be sensitive to any children with disabilities.

Main activity: Baby photos
You may like to ask children to bring in photos of when they were young. What has changed? Emphasise that we all grow and change as we grow older. Sometimes staff are willing to show pictures of themselves as babies/toddlers and it can be fun for the class to try to guess who the pictures are. Thinking ahead, what will change in the future?

Reflection/plenary
Ask children to reflect on what they are looking forward to when they grow up and to complete the sentence 'When I'm older I will be able to ...'

Differentiation
As with the previous lesson, there will be a wide range of maturity within your class.

- *Children needing more of a challenge* – could identify ways in which they have become more responsible as they have got older.
- *Children with additional learning needs* – could continue to explore how they have changed since they were a baby.

What if ...
There is a child with a physical disability in the class? It is important to remind the class that although there are many similarities between us we are also all different and special in our own way.

Male and female (Key Stage 2)

This lesson builds on the body parts lesson in Key Stage 1 and the children label a life-size diagram with the names of internal body organs. They look at drawings or diagrams of male and female reproductive organs and learn how they relate to things that will happen to them. They brainstorm names they are familiar with for sexual body parts, learn to understand what they mean and about their appropriate use. This lesson supports the Science curriculum. Teachers may need to check whether the representation of the human body is acceptable to parents/carers of different faiths in the class. (The school's SRE policy should address this. It might be that working in single-gender groups on this activity will address some faith concerns.)

By the end of this lesson pupils will be able to identify parts of the reproductive system in males and females and describe their functions. They will also have considered appropriate terminology for use in different contexts.

Learning outcomes
- I know what my main internal and external organs do.
- I can identify body parts that are different between boys and girls.
- I can identify body parts that are the same in boys and girls.

Working agreement
Remind the children about the working agreement, emphasise the importance of treating each other with respect and about the need to think before talking about personal matters with the whole group.

Resources needed
- Accurate representations of male and female bodies including reproductive organs.
- Large pieces of paper, pens, tape, glue and modelling materials, including plasticine, string and cardboard tubes.

Opening activity: Ping pong
Ask the children to form pairs, standing facing each other. They are going to take turns to say words and try to develop a rhythm, like batting a tennis ball back and forth. Demonstrate with an easy one, like the names of trees. Now give the pairs these categories one at a time: clothes; names of body parts under the clothes; names of body parts under the skin.

Main activity: Language activity
In small groups ask the children to write down *any* words they know or have heard for sexual body parts in two columns labelled 'Boys' and 'Girls'. Teachers to stick the paper up on the walls and talk about the words. Make sure children know how they relate to the correct medical terms – vagina, womb, ovaries, fallopian tubes, clitoris, vulva, labia, penis, testes, scrotum and urethra. Talk about how we need to use different words in different situations and with different people – at home, in public places, at school and with health staff.

Main activity: Model-making

You will need accurate representations of the human reproductive organs in males and females – make sure the children understand how they relate to the body as a whole (sometimes disembodied organs are difficult to understand). Many SRE packs, videos and anatomical models are available, or you can draw your own. In small, single-gender groups, give each group three different representations of either a male or female reproductive system. Ask them to study the pictures and then make a 3D model of the reproductive organs using the materials provided, for example plasticine, string, fabric, straws, sticky tape, ping pong balls etc. Ask a volunteer from each group to briefly describe their model. Summarise by correctly describing the functions of the different parts in the context of growing up and becoming an adult. Answer questions.

Reflection/plenary

Go round the class asking children to complete the sentence, 'One thing I've learnt today that I didn't know before is …'

Differentiation

- *Children needing more of a challenge* – could make a body 'dictionary' with accurate descriptions of the functions of the major organs, including the reproductive system.
- *Children with additional learning needs* – may find understanding the concept of 'what is inside our bodies' quite difficult, so you might want to work with small groups of children to explain it more fully. Make aprons displaying pictures of actual (child-) sized organs (with adult support) as this enhances children's understanding of how things 'fit together' (you can also buy these from science education catalogues).

What if …

- *Someone says, I've seen my dad's willy?* You'll probably want to refer to the point in the class working agreement about talking about personal matters and protecting other people's privacy. Point out to the class that talking about personal things isn't always a good idea but that, if someone has any kind of problem or question, you're always there to listen. (Remember also to explain the limits of the confidentiality school staff can offer.) You should consider using a 'question box' for anonymous questions.
- *Being naked?* You may want to reflect with the class that in our homes we may feel comfortable to walk around naked, but explore with them times when it is not appropriate to walk around naked. If you have any suspicion that this may be an abuse situation, you should talk to the child protection member of staff.

Growing and changing
(Key Stage 2, Part 1 – Years 3 and 4)

By the end of this lesson pupils have thought about how they have grown and changed and how they will grow and change in the future. They will be able to identify the external physical changes that happen to their bodies as they grow to adulthood, and know that when the body starts to change this is called puberty.

Learning outcomes
Years 3 and 4: I can tell you the main physical changes that take place during puberty.

Working agreement
Remind the children about the working agreement and emphasise the rules about treating each other with respect and avoiding sharing personal information or asking personal questions. Remind them of who they can talk with (school staff, parents/carers, school nurse) if they have questions. Remind pupils of how the question box works and the limits of school staff confidentiality.

Resources needed
- For each group, a large sheet of paper for a timeline and sets of pictures of males and females of different ages involved in different activities.
- Simple drawings of a naked girl and a woman and a boy and a man from a published scheme, magazines or the internet.

Opening activity: Timeline
Put the class into small groups and give them a selection of pictures of both males and females and ask them to put them into a timeline showing how they have grown and changed since babyhood to the present day, with a focus on physical abilities (for example, movement milestones like sit, crawl, walk, run, jump, climb, cycle, kick a ball, swim and so forth). Be sensitive to the range of ability and any children with disabilities. When the children have completed this, ask them to note on their timelines ways in which they have been given more responsibility as they grew up.

Main activity: Simple drawings
In pairs or small groups, look at simple drawings of a naked girl and a woman and a boy and a man. How has an adult woman/man's body changed? How is a grown-up body different from the child's body? Ask for feedback. Reinforce the use of scientific language for the body parts that are linked to sexual reproduction (parts of the body important for sex and if people choose to have a baby when they are grown up). Accept family names but talk about the aim to use scientific names. Highlight why use of this language is important (because it is universal and so on).

Explain that one of the major body changes that we go through is called puberty. Ask the children what they know already about puberty and what happens to our bodies as we start to grow up? Rectify any misconceptions from prior knowledge/discussion and answer any further questions.

Reflection/plenary

Ask the children to draw two pictures side by side, one of themselves as they are now and one showing themselves at the age of 20. They can label the drawings to show the changes that will have taken place, not only physically but also changes in relationships, interests, responsibilities and new things that they will be able to do.

Differentiation

As with the previous lesson, there will be a wide range of maturity within the class, with some children already experiencing pubertal changes.

- *Children needing more of a challenge* – could create their own booklets about changes in puberty.
- *Children with additional learning needs* – could do further work in small groups to draw, on body outlines, the changes that happen to boys and girls at puberty.

What if …

- *Children who either are not very physically developed or perhaps are quite developed are singled out for ridicule?* The class working agreement is very important here and should have something to say about not making personal remarks. In addition, point out that children go through these changes at different rates and that this is quite normal.

Puberty (Key Stage 2, Part 2 – Years 5 and 6)

By the end of this lesson pupils will know and understand about the physical and emotional changes that take place at puberty.

Learning outcomes
- I understand that my body may change at a different rate to those of my friends.
- I know that I am likely to experience mood swings during puberty.
- I understand what menstruation is.
- I can explain the changes that will take place in girls' and boys' bodies during puberty. I understand what wet dreams are.
- I am learning how to manage changes and puberty and support others to do the same.

Working agreement
Remind the children about the working agreement and emphasise the rules about treating each other with respect and avoiding sharing personal information or asking personal questions. Remind them of who they can talk with (school staff, parents/carers, school nurse) if they have questions. Remind pupils of how the question box works and the limits of school staff confidentiality.

Resources needed
- Sets of 'Changes at puberty' cards.
- Books, leaflets or a DVD providing information to boys and girls about the physical and emotional changes at puberty.
- Slips of paper and a hat.

Opening activity: Mix 'n' match and line-ups
- Clear a space in the classroom so that pupils can stand in it and move around freely.
- Ask them to form groups according to eye colour, favourite food, number in the family, favourite subject, hobbies and so forth.
- Ask them to line up according to height, birthday, shoe size, hair or skin colour.
- Have they found themselves always in the same groups and at the same point in the line-ups? What can they conclude?
- Emphasise that everybody is unique and yet we have similarities.

Main activity: Card sort
In mixed groups, ask the children to look at a selection of 'Changes at puberty' cards. Ask the children to put the cards into three piles: (a) the changes that happen to girls, (b) the changes that happen to boys and (c) the changes that happen to both. Discuss their choices and check understanding of changes relating to different genders. Remind them that while some of them will already be experiencing these changes others will experience them in the future. Reassure them that this variation is completely normal.

Main activity: Lucky dip
Split into girls and boys.

Girls: Give each girl a slip of paper and ask them to write down a question they have about changes that will happen to them at puberty, and then fold it up. Collect the slips in a hat, mix them up and pass round the hat so that each girl can take one out. Ask the girls to read out what is on their paper and make a list of the questions on the flip chart.

Give out and, in pairs, ask them to find the answers to the group's questions. Give each pair a book or leaflet with information about puberty in girls (or show the relevant section of the DVD to all the girls). Go through their answers with the group as a whole, and ask:

- if they have discovered anything else about puberty in girls
- if all the changes at puberty are physical (there will be changes in feelings too)
- when do these changes start and how long will they take, and do all girls experience them at the same time
- if they have any new questions.

Now ask the pairs to join with another pair to form fours to discuss questions they would like to ask the boys about puberty. Ask the groups to write one of the questions on the flip chart in turn, avoiding duplicate questions. Assign one question to each of the groups.

Boys: Repeat the above exercise with the boys' group, substituting a book or leaflet designed to look at puberty for boys (or showing the relevant section of a DVD). End with the groups coming up with a list of questions to ask the girls about puberty.

Bring the boys' and girls' groups back together with their lists of questions. Starting with the boys' questions, each small group of boys asks one question, which is answered by one of the girls' groups. When all the boys' questions have been answered, use the same process to put and respond to the girls' questions for the boys.

It may help to answer questions about menstruation to have prepared a small cup half-filled with some coloured liquid to demonstrate how much blood is released in the menstrual flow. Remind the children that this takes place over several days. You may also wish to have a 5ml spoon or similar and some liquid to illustrate how small the amount of liquid is that contains several million sperm.

Discuss similarities and differences in puberty in girls and boys, including both the physical and emotional changes. Emphasise that puberty is a natural and normal part of everybody's life and that you should talk to an adult if there is anything that worries you. Emphasise that these changes happen to everyone but they don't happen to everyone at the same time.

Reflection/plenary

- Something that has surprised them in the lesson ...
- Something they would like to know more about ...
- Follow-up – note that girls may need a separate lesson to discuss menstruation, to understand more about the menstrual cycle and to investigate a selection of sanitary protection.

Differentiation

As with the previous lesson, there will be a wide range of maturity within the class, with some children already experiencing pubertal changes.

- *Children needing more of a challenge* – could create their own booklets about changes in puberty.
- *Children with additional learning needs* – could do further work in small groups to draw, on body outlines, the changes that happen to boys and girls at puberty.

What if ...

Children who either are not very physically developed or perhaps are quite developed are singled out for ridicule? The class working agreement is very important here and should have something to say about not making personal remarks.

Sample assessment activities

Learning outcome	Assessment activity
- I can label boys' and girls' body parts. - I can tell you my family word for boys' and girls' parts and what the biological name is for this part of the body.	With the support of a teaching assistant, work with individual children or small groups of children to ask them to tell you about the body parts of a cartoon child or a photograph of a baby. Prompt pupils to tell you the words for penis and vagina. Record pupils as having met or working towards the learning outcome.
- I know what my main internal and external organs do. - I can identify body parts that are different between boys and girls. - I can identify body parts that are the same in boys and girls.	Ask pupils to match words of the body parts to definitions and then to sort into groups according to whether they are male or female or both. Assess these against the learning outcomes to identify any further learning needs.
- I can tell you the main physical changes that take place during puberty.	Ask pupils to list all the changes that take place during puberty and to group them according to whether they are changes that happen for boys, girls or both. Assess their work according to whether they are working at, towards or beyond the expected level.

Theme 2: Life cycles

Introduction

Reproduction

As part of any primary school sciences curriculum, children should develop an understanding that animals, including humans reproduce and that humans produce babies and these babies grow into children and then into adults. The SRE aspects of PSHE education could include supportive work on the needs of children and families, parental responsibilities and how to get help.

In response to children's questions like, 'Do you have to have babies?', teachers can introduce the concept that adults are able to make decisions about whether or not to have a baby. The responsibilities of parenthood and the needs of very young children can be emphasised.

In Years 3 to 6, children are approaching or entering puberty. The Science Curriculum should include teaching about the main stages of the human life cycle (At the time of writing this was included in the National Curriculum QCA 1999a). This involves an understanding of the beginning of fertility, conception and the process of contraception, which can be explained within a family context. Children will often have heard about contraception and may have seen contraception at home. Once older children understand the basic concepts of sexual reproduction, including conception, they can consider how conception might be prevented – that is, by a barrier or by preventing fertilisation or implantation. It is not necessary to teach about the range of contraceptives available.

Work on friendships, relationships and morality, peer pressure, influence and making choices are all part of developing the skills children will need as they grow up. These skills are all-important for later teaching about contraception, as confidence and good self-esteem are fundamental to taking sexual and reproductive health issues seriously in the future.

Note we do not include here a dedicated Key Stage 1 lesson plan on human reproduction. The preparation for this is covered in 'Theme 1: My body' in Key Stage 1.

Key questions on 'Life cycles'

Years 1 and 2
- Where do babies come from?
- How much have I changed since I was a baby?
- How are other children similar and different to me?

Years 3 and 4
- Why does having a baby need a male and a female?
- What are eggs and sperm?
- How do different animals have babies?
- How do different animals look after their babies before and after birth?
- What happens when people get older?

Years 5 and 6
- What is sex?
- What is sexual intercourse?
- How many sperm does a man produce?
- How many eggs does a woman have?
- How do sperm reach the egg to make a baby?
- Does conception always occur or can it be prevented?
- How do families with same-sex parents have babies?
- How does the baby develop?
- How is the baby born?
- What does a new baby need to keep it happy and healthy?

Brief summary of sexual reproduction

Before explaining reproduction it is important to recap on the differences between male and female, emphasising the correct names of the reproductive organs, including penis and vagina.

Emphasise that all animals have babies and that in humans, an adult male and adult female make a baby when they are ready through 'sexual intercourse'. Explain that sexual intercourse is when a man and a woman join together and the man puts his penis inside the woman's vagina. The penis then produces a small seed called a sperm which swims up and joins an egg (called an ovum) inside the woman's body.

Caring for babies and children (Key Stage 1)

By the end of this lesson pupils will understand what babies need in order to be happy and healthy, understand the demands of looking after a baby and think about how they can help care for babies and young children they know.

Learning outcomes
I know what a new baby needs.

Working agreement
Remind the children about the working agreement and emphasise the importance of respecting differences between individuals and families.

Resources needed
- Flip chart or whiteboard
- Selection of baby objects (see activity for examples)
- Pictures of babies and toddlers at different stages of development
- Babycare catalogues
- Bags of flour.

Opening activity: Pass the baby
Using a bag of flour (or something big enough for two hands to hold), which you are pretending to be a baby, have it passed carefully round the circle using two hands. Ask the children to say how they felt holding the 'baby'.

Main activity: Baby objects carousel
Organise into groups of five and talk about what it would be like to have a new baby in the family.

Set up tables with selections of objects or pictures, each table focusing on a different aspect – for example, baby clothes, feeding equipment, nappies, toys, baby books and so forth. Ask the children in small groups to visit each of the tables and come up with three things that parents/carers need to do to look after their newborn child. Is there anything missing? Is there anything else you can think of? Ask the groups for feedback.

Discuss all the ways in which babies need to be kept physically safe and healthy (warmth, food, to be kept clean, a secure environment with no dangers) and all the ways babies need to be helped to develop emotionally and intellectually (love, affection, play, reading, company, fun).

Lead the children into a discussion of all the things parents/carers have to be able to do to bring up a baby to be healthy and safe. Record these ideas on a flip chart or whiteboard around a picture of a young baby and a toddler. Emphasise how much time it takes to look after a baby and how important it is for babies to be loved and played with as well as being clothed and fed.

Reflection/plenary

Go round the class asking children to say what they could do to help look after a baby or a toddler. Remind them that a baby always needs an adult around and that they should always ask an adult before doing anything with a baby.

Differentiation

- *Children needing more of a challenge* – could design a mobile, pram rattle or a book for a baby or toddler.
- *Children with additional learning needs* – could make a collage, using images from babycare catalogues showing all the things babies and toddlers need at different stages.

What if ...

Someone says, 'I don't like my baby sister because she cries in the night and wakes me up'. Explain how difficult it can be when babies cry for long periods, especially in the middle of the night, and that the whole family may be disturbed. Explain that the baby isn't doing it on purpose and that it can't help crying. Crying is the only way a little baby can communicate. It is important not to be angry with babies, but give them lots of love and cuddles.

Caring for babies and children (Key Stage 2)

By the end of this lesson pupils will understand what babies need in order to be happy and healthy, understand the demands of looking after a baby and think about how they can help care for babies and young children they know.

Learning outcomes
- I know what is involved in looking after a baby.
- I can describe the changes having a new baby in the family can bring.

Working agreement
Remind the children about the working agreement and emphasise the importance of respecting differences between individuals and families.

Resources needed
- Flip chart or whiteboard
- *Flour Babies* by Ann Fine (for additional activity)
- Human bingo grids.

Opening activity: Human bingo
Give each pupil a grid with six squares with six questions, such as find someone who has seen a newborn baby, someone who knows someone who is pregnant, someone who has sisters/brothers, someone who has bathed a baby and so on. The first person to complete the grid with a different name in each box shouts 'Bingo!'

Main activity: Meet the visitor
Invite a parent/carer to come in and talk to the class about the impact of a baby on their lives.

Part 1: Preparing for a visitor
This is an opportunity to give the class some responsibility for managing the visit. Give some time for preparation so that the class can think about the following questions. How shall we:

- make the visitor feel comfortable?
- arrange the room?
- collect the visitor?
- introduce ourselves?
- decide what questions to ask?
- keep to time?
- end the session?
- thank the visitor and escort them out?

Note that it is important to check with the visitor that they are comfortable with the class taking charge of the session in this way. It may be possible to arrange for the class to divide into two or three smaller groups, each with their own parent/carer visitor.

Part 2: Meeting the visitor
The class carries out their plan and the teacher observes and does not contribute, allowing the class real responsibility for the parent.

Reflection/plenary
The class discusses what they learnt from the parent and also how well they managed the visit, identifying things that went well and any changes they would make when they have another visitor to the class.

Reflect on: all the things that babies can and cannot do and need help with; how dependent they are on people to care for them; physical changes in the house; new equipment; less room; noise levels; parents/carers roles/ jobs changing; childcare for other siblings; baby crying; tired parents; lots of visitors; parties; christenings and so on.

Follow-up activity
Teachers may like to get the class to look after an egg (hardboiled – or uncooked if you are brave enough) or a bag of flour as if it were a baby for a day or a week. Children can draw or paint a face and make a cradle and a shawl for their 'baby'. Just as if it were a real baby, it must not be left alone and must be treated very carefully at all times (so that it doesn't break or leak). After the set time, discuss how they felt about having this responsibility. The novel *Flour Babies* by Anne Fine describes how a boy had to do this at school and the emotions he experiences.

Differentiation
- *Children needing more of a challenge* – could design a mobile, pram rattle or a book for a baby or toddler.
- *Children with additional learning needs* – could make a collage, using images from baby care catalogues showing all the things babies and toddlers need at different stages.

What if ...
Someone says, 'When my baby brother cries my mum gets really cross'?
Explain how difficult it can be when babies cry for long periods, especially in the middle of the night, and that parents/carers can sometimes find it overwhelming and like any of us lose their temper. Explain that the baby isn't doing it on purpose and that it can't help crying. Say that a health visitor or a GP may be able to suggest things that can help.

Sample assessment activities

Learning outcome	Assessment activity
I know what a baby needs.	Draw and write: On a large piece of paper ask the children to draw a baby in the middle, then brainstorm what a baby needs, writing or drawing around the baby.
I can describe the changes having a new baby in the family can bring.	Role play: In pairs or small groups plan and present a role play illustrating the impact a new baby has on the family.
I know how a baby starts to grow.	Sorting activity: Individually or in pairs give children cards with images of the different stages of a baby's development, including fertilisation, stages in the womb and after it is born. Ask the children to put them into the right order.

Life cycles and reproduction (Key Stage 2, early – Years 3 and 4)

By the end of this lesson children will have a basic understanding that animals and humans have babies. They will have a basic understanding of human reproduction. This lesson will be linked with the Science Curriculum.

Learning outcomes
- I know how different animals produce their young.
- I know that sexual reproduction involves a male and a female cell joining together; this is called fertilisation.
- I know how a baby starts to grow.
- I can tell you how a baby is born.

Working agreement
Recap ground rules and remind children how to use the question box.

Resources needed
- Animal jigsaws
- Sets of cards showing pictures of baby animals and their mothers, including fish, frogs, reptiles, birds, mammals and humans.

Opening activity: Animal family jigsaws
Cut up pictures of animals, preferably with their young, into four or five pieces to make a jigsaw. (Magazines and calendars are a good source of animal pictures.) Mix up all the picture pieces in a hat or box and ask each child to take one; there should be the same number of pieces as children in the class. Ask the children to find and join up their pieces to make the complete picture, forming a small group.

Main activity: Matching baby with the carer
Give each small group a set of cards showing pictures of baby animals and their mothers, including fish, frogs, reptiles, birds, mammals and humans. Ask them to match the mothers with their babies. Does the baby have a different name to the mother – for example, tadpole and frog?

Ask them to look for similarities and differences in the way that animals, including humans, produce young. Emphasise the following points: male and female; eggs and sperm; numbers of eggs and sperm produced; fertilisation in water and on land; eggs developing in water; in a shell or in a body; numbers of babies produced; survival rates and levels of parental care; leading towards an understanding that humans produce fewer offspring as they are cared for in loving relationships.

Reflection/plenary
Make a class display showing the main types of sexual reproduction in animals.

Differentiation
- *Children needing more of a challenge* – could draw the basic life cycles of various animals, e.g. egg to chicken, tadpole to frog, baby human to adult human.
- *Children with additional learning needs* – may need further opportunities to talk through the activity mentioned above, perhaps concentrating on one animal, in a small group with a learning assistant.

What if …
A child asks about fertilisation in humans? Seeing human reproduction in the context of animal adaptations to reproduction provides an opportunity to explain that the male penis has evolved in mammals as a means to transfer sperm to the female in the dry environment on land. Even aquatic mammals like seals and whales reproduce like this rather than like fish.

Reproduction and birth
(Key Stage 2 – Years 5 and 6)

By the end of this lesson pupils will know and understand about the processes of reproduction and birth as part of the human life cycle. Questions may arise about contraception, and follow-up work may need to be done to address this issue.

Learning outcomes
- I understand how pregnancy happens and I understand that pregnancy can be prevented.
- I can tell you what the age of consent is.

Working agreement
Remind the children about the working agreement and emphasise the rule about treating each other with respect.

Resources needed
- Whiteboard/flip chart.
- Unlabelled pictures (one per pupil) of the following: male external genitalia; female external genitalia; male reproductive organs; female reproductive system; baby developing in the uterus.
- DVD/interactive whiteboard resource or other visual aid – for example, pictures showing the main stages of human reproduction, conception, foetal development and birth.
- Materials for reinforcement activity (quiz, sequencing pictures, word match, true/false).

Opening activity: Picture groups
Give each pupil an unlabelled picture of one of the following: male external genitalia; female external genitalia; male reproductive organs; female reproductive system; baby developing in the uterus. Ask them to find pupils with the same picture and see if they can name all the parts and say what they do. Tell them to keep their pictures until the end of the lesson when they can add any terms they have learnt.

Main activity: Viewing an audio-visual aid
Recap on previous lessons on animal reproduction and explain that the focus of the lesson today is on how human beings reproduce. You may want to use a video, DVD or other audio-visual aid to help with this lesson. (See the 'Choosing resources' section on page 30.) Reference books for children will also help teachers find appropriate wording to describe sexual intercourse. Set the context by explaining that having sexual intercourse (sex) is the main way a new baby is created or conceived. Explain that adults also express loving feelings for each other through sex.

If pupils have previously learnt about animal life cycles, it is not always necessary to show images or diagrams of human sexual intercourse. Refer to the schools SRE policy, which should have considered parents' views on the images to be used. There is a great variety of good visual material available. Schools and parents' can choose what would be most suitable and understandable for their children.

Explain as simply as you can the process of having sex, being pregnant and giving birth. You may want to follow each of the explanations with an age-appropriate DVD clip and activity.

Check on how much the children have learnt and understood by following up the visual presentation by giving the class one of the following activities to be carried out in small groups:

- a quiz
- a sequencing activity – for example, put pictures of stages in conception and implantation in the correct order
- matching terminology on cards with the correct definitions
- a true–false activity, such as sorting statements on cards or children in the whole class moving to the 'true' or 'false' side of the room in response to each statement.

When delivering this content in Years 5 and 6 it will be appropriate to explain briefly that if the couple do not want to have a baby they can use contraception, such as the pill or condoms. Pupils may ask follow-up questions about this and so have some responses prepared that include the different faith perspectives on contraception.

Pupils, particularly in upper Key Stage 2, are often curious about multiple births, and other methods of conception such as fertility treatment. Prepare responses that do not detract from the key learning outcomes from the lesson.

Ensure there is some acknowledgement of the different ways that children come into families; including adoption, fostering and fertility treatment. In Years 5 and 6 this may include teaching about how same-sex couples have families.

Reflection/plenary
Ask the groups of pupils to revisit their pictures from the opening activity and add new terms and functions.

Get children to write any questions they have as a result of this lesson on pieces of paper and put them anonymously into a box to be answered at the start of the next lesson. Seek support from the PSHE education coordinator and/or the school nurse to answer these questions. It may be appropriate to type out some of the questions and ask pupils to come up with responses. Read an age-appropriate story/picture book. If specific questions about contraception arise, a follow-up lesson may need to be developed.

Differentiation

Children in the class will be more or less ready to learn that sexual intercourse can lead to conception, depending on their maturity and backgrounds, so you need to be aware of the range of their prior knowledge and likely exposure to sexual situations, which could include TV soaps, soft porn videos or real situations. Use their questions or a needs assessment activity to gauge the detail that they require. A straightforward needs assessment activity could be to simply ask children in groups to list all the ways they know that a baby can come into a family.

- *Children needing more of a challenge* – could write an explanation of how humans reproduce for a creature from another planet to read.
- *Children with additional learning needs* – may need further opportunities to read and talk through one of the books mentioned above in a small group with a learning assistant.

What if …

Questions in the box are silly or offensive? It is important for teachers to model that it is alright to talk about sex and so answering some of these questions in an age-appropriate way can give this impression. You could also explore with the class why some of us might ask 'silly' questions – is it because of embarrassment? Some questions may not be age appropriate to answer. A teacher may be able to identify who has written the question and can follow it up with the individual as appropriate. Be aware that a question may reveal a fundamental lack of understanding that the teacher may need to address or an inappropriate comment that may need to be challenged generally within an activity.

Theme 3: Relationships

Introduction

Work on relationships in SRE is vital because it puts the learning on life cycles, puberty and reproduction into a human context. While it is important for children to know about the biology of human reproduction, they are also keen to learn about the changes in relationships that growing up brings. This theme will explore friendships and families of all kinds.

Friendships

Work on friendships could be said to be the key to good SRE. If children are given opportunities to consider what makes a good friend and understand why they are attracted to some people rather than others, then they have the basis for developing good sexual relationships later on. This will also help with developing empathy, being tolerant of differences and not having unrealistic expectations of others. Conflict resolution and dealing with bullying is something that all schools need to address.

Primary school teachers know that the ups and downs of friendships between children are the stuff of everyday life in school and that most children will have experienced many different aspects of friendship. Finding ways to discuss these things without using personal examples can be achieved in PSHE education and SRE using children's literature, discussion, circle time, puppets, drama and case studies. All children should be aware of the school's anti-bullying strategy and where to go for help.

Families of all kinds

Children need to have opportunities to explore different relationships – including families, friendships, partnerships and marriage – and by doing this to learn to value diversity. This is an area that children and young people report as often missing from their formal SRE (DfEE 2000). Children learn more about marriage and relationships from their own homes than they do from anywhere else (The National Society 2002) and these experiences provide powerful messages about how people manage relationships and behave towards others.

For some children, what they have learnt from their parents' or family members' relationships and marriages will be predominantly positive, but for others: 'it will be painful or unpredictable, confused and confusing. For some children, neglect or abuse will be what they know of relationships' (The National Society 2002). It is vital, therefore, that schools should explicitly address this area of children's learning while showing sensitivity to different experiences. It is important to emphasise that a person's need to be loved and cared for is initially met by the family but it is also met by others, including friends, teachers and other adults. Some children may experience more care and love from people such as foster carers and social workers.

SRE also needs to reflect the realities of children's very different lives. This will include children whose parents are married, those who are not married, children whose parents have divorced or separated, single parent families, children in public care and children looked after by grandparents, mixed-race parents, disabled parents and same-sex parents. Diverse family groupings should be represented and affirmed within the SRE resources used. In this respect, children's fiction is particularly useful.

Children from a young age will also be aware of and ask questions related to the range of sexual orientations that they are aware of through their families, the media and the community they live in. Lesbian, gay and bisexual sexual orientations should be discussed in terms of family diversity, marriage and civil partnerships and, for Key Stage 2, with the recognition that people can feel attracted to the opposite sex, the same sex or both. It should also be covered in work to challenge homophobia. Links to the school's anti-bullying policy should be made.

Within the context of talking about relationships, children should be taught about the nature of marriage and its importance for family life and for bringing up children. The government recognises that there are strong and mutually supportive relationships outside marriage. Therefore, children should learn the significance of marriage and stable relationships as key building blocks of community and society. Teaching in this area needs to be sensitive so as not to stigmatise children on the basis of their home circumstances.

> Only 6 out of 32 children in my class live in a conventional family with both parents. If I went down the route of talking only about marriage I would not be addressing the needs of 26 of my pupils.
> Deputy headteacher

Key questions on 'Relationships'

Early primary
- Who is in my family?
- How are other families similar or different to mine?
- What does my family do for me?
- What do I like about my friend?
- What does my friend like about me?
- What can other people do to make me feel good?
- Who do I look after?
- Why shouldn't I tease other people?

Middle primary
- How have my relationships changed as I have grown up?
- Why do friendships change?
- How can I be a good friend?
- Why can it be fun to have a friend who is different to me?
- What are some of the bad ways people can behave towards one another?
- How do I know when I am being bullied?
- What do I do if I am being bullied?
- How can I make up with my friend when we have fallen out?
- Why are some parents married and some not?

Late primary
- What are the important relationships in my life now?
- What is love? How do we show love to one another?
- Can people of the same sex love one another? Is this alright?
- What are the different kinds of families and partnerships?
- What do the words 'lesbian' and 'gay' mean?
- Why does calling someone 'gay' count as bullying?
- What should I do if someone is being bullied or abused?
- Are boys and girls expected to behave differently in relationships? Why?
- Can some relationships be harmful?
- Why are families important for having babies and bringing them up?

Similarities and differences (Key Stage 1)

By the end of this lesson the children will recognise similarities and differences between themselves and others, learn that their actions have an impact on other people and be able to identify ways in which they are special.

Learning outcomes
- I can tell you how I am the same as and different from my friends.
- I am proud of the ways in which I am different.
- I know that there are similarities and differences between every child in the class.

Working agreement
Remind the children of the working agreement and emphasise the need to treat everyone with respect.

Resources needed
- Materials for drawing or painting portraits or writing materials.
- Puppet or soft toy.

Opening activity: All change
Invite the children to form a circle, then ask them to stand up and change places if they have long/short hair, shoes with Velcro/buckles, like the colour blue/pink, have a birthday in a certain month and so on. Invite the children to form pairs, then ask them to find out two things they have in common and two things that are different and to tell the rest of the group about them. (For example, 'We both have blue eyes but I am right handed and you are left handed.') Comment on how there are lots of ways that we are the same but lots of ways that we are special and different from each other.

Main activity: Portraits
Ask the children to draw or paint portraits of each other making them as detailed as possible, and then ask them to write down three things that make that person special. Next, ask the children whether they can identify others from the portraits and/or descriptions? Stress that we are all unique and there is no-one else quite like us. You could invite them to go on to think about the ways in which we are the same (for example, we all need food and drink and sleep, we all feel sad if someone is nasty to us, we all like to play).

Introduce a puppet or soft toy. Work with the children to make up a scenario about a puppet who is different because of the way 'he' or 'she' looks (for example, because they have glasses, freckles or are small/tall). Talk about how the character feels when people are nasty to them because they're different.

If appropriate to the age and understanding of the group, remind them of the school's anti-bullying policy and that it can be particularly hurtful to pick on or tease others because of their differences.

Reflection/plenary
Go round the class asking children to complete the sentence, 'The person next to me is special because …' (the teacher should illustrate this with an example).

Differentiation
- *Children needing more of a challenge* – could write detailed descriptions of each other's appearance and characteristics.
- *Children with additional learning needs* – could use mirrors to help make accurate representations of their faces. They can then use digital cameras to compare and contrast their images.

What if …
There is a child in the class who is often picked on because of their appearance? Make sure you remind the class of the working agreement throughout the activities. Distance the learning by focusing on the puppet and getting the children to think about how it feels to be laughed at. Make reference to the school's position on bullying.

Gender stereotypes (Key Stage 1)

By the end of this lesson, the children will know the physical differences between boys and girls, be able to think about other 'differences' between girls and boys and where these (stereotypes) come from, and begin to question whether children have to conform to gender stereotypes. This lesson is linked to the Key Stage 1 'Male and female' lesson in the 'My body' theme.

Learning outcomes
- I understand that boys and girls can have lots of similarities.
- I understand that boys and girls can like both the same and different things and that this is alright.
- I know that it is wrong to tease someone because they are different.

Working agreement
Remind the children of the working agreement and emphasise the importance of listening carefully to each other and respecting different viewpoints.

Resources needed
- Large picture of a baby
- Whiteboard or flip chart
- Paper, pencils and colouring materials
- Selection of toys, toy catalogue or pictures of toys
- Scissors.

Opening activity: Baby picture
Find a picture of a baby whose gender is not immediately obvious. Ask the children to suggest a name for the baby. They could do this in pairs, small groups or you could take suggestions from the whole group. If they ask, 'Is the baby a boy or a girl?', tell them you don't know. If they simply suggest names, ask them why they are assuming if it is a boy or a girl (there will probably be some statements made that you can explore). Remind them that there are physical differences that they have learnt in a previous lesson on the differences between males and females, but today they will be looking at other differences.

Main activity: Picture sort
In small groups, using a wide range of pictures of toys, ask the children to sort the pictures into three categories: toys for girls, toys for boys and toys for both.

As a whole class, discuss which toys are for boys/girls and challenge their thinking.

Reflection/plenary
Read the children a story that challenges gender stereotypes, such as the *Paper Bag Princess* or any of Allan Ahlberg's *Happy Families* series, and

talk about how the characters are behaving in a way that we might not expect a male or a female to behave.

Differentiation
- *Children needing more of a challenge* – ask them to consider why they think people tend to believe that girls like pink, and so on. Some toy catalogues might help them to explore this.
- *Children with additional learning needs* – could work with a teaching assistant or other helper to look through a toy catalogue and choose and cut out pictures of toys that boys and girls would both enjoy playing with. At the same time they could continue talking about differences and similarities.

Follow-up activity
You could extend the discussion in the main activity into a wider discussion about men and women and their different roles – particularly around the house and in caring for children – and to the different jobs men and women do. Try to challenge the children's views that these differences are inevitable and be ready to suggest jobs that are done by both sexes (such as bus drivers, soldiers, astronauts, postal deliveries, nurses, doctors).

There are a range of resources that look specifically at gender such as Women's Aid Expect Respect resource' – http://www.womensaid.org.uk.

What if …
A child comments, 'My Dad says that boys don't cry'? Explain that anyone might cry if they get hurt or feel very sad or upset and that crying is a natural way of showing your feelings. Ask the children if there is anyone who has never cried. Explain that there are some people who think that boys and men should always be strong and never show if they are hurt or sad, but that it is perfectly natural to cry, that it will help you start to feel better and that if other people see you crying they will know you need help.

Caring (Key Stage 1)

By the end of this lesson children will know and understand why families are special for caring and sharing, and understand how their feelings and actions have an impact on other people. This lesson can be linked with the lessons on 'Caring for babies' on page 78.

Learning outcomes
- I can give examples of how special people in my life look after me.
- I can explain how I show I care about others.

Working agreement
Remind the children of the working agreement and emphasise that we are all special and should listen to each other.

Resources needed
A pet or a picture of a pet.

Opening activity: Car wash
Form the class into two lines facing each other. Ask for a volunteer to go through the 'car wash'. As they walk through, everyone pats them gently. Once they reach the end they join a line and another pupil goes through the wash. Ask the volunteers how it felt. Was it a nice feeling? Did people pat them carefully?

Main activity: Caring for a pet
Using a real pet or a picture of a pet, ask the children to think about, 'How do we care for a pet?' Discuss the different needs and include physical, social and emotional needs. Now ask the class to think about people. How do people care for us? And who are the people who care for us?

Reflection/plenary
Ask the children to think about something – for example, an animal, plant or person – they have looked after, and to share one thing that they did to look after it.

Differentiation
- *Children needing more of a challenge* – could design and write a greeting card to say thank you to one of their special people for everything they do to help and look after them.
- *Children with additional learning needs* – could design a card as above and dictate the greeting to the learning assistant to type and print on the computer, or choose a ready-printed greeting.

What if ...
A child gets very upset because their parents have just split up? Tell them that it is alright to feel sad and remind them of other special people in their lives. Tell them that it is good to talk about feelings and let them know that you will always try to find time to listen. You may be able to find another

child in the school who has gone through the same experience who could be a special buddy. You could also find a storybook about children whose parents have separated.

Friends (Key Stage 1)

By the end of this lesson the children will have thought about what makes a friend, be able to talk with someone about themselves, and understand how their feelings and actions have an impact on other people. The focus of this class is developing listening skills.

Learning outcomes
- I can listen well and learn new things about someone else.
- I can identify the qualities of a good friend.
- I can demonstrate some of the skills needed to make and maintain friendships.

Working agreement
Remind the children of the working agreement and emphasise the importance of treating each other kindly.

Resources needed
- Paper and drawing materials for posters
- Puppet or soft toy.

Opening activity: There's a space on my right

The children sit in a circle with one extra space or chair. The child with the empty space on their right says, 'There a space on my right and I would like … to sit in it.' The chosen person sits in the space, leaving their chair empty. The person who now has the empty space to their right repeats the sentence. Repeat six times. Ask the children to think of a rule to make sure everybody gets a turn and discuss the importance of fairness.

Main activity: Listening activity
Ask the children to call out what makes a good friend – for example, someone who is kind, who listens, who plays with them or who gives them a hug when they are sad. Make a list. Choosing 'Who listens' tell the class they will now be practising 'good listening' with one another.

In pairs, preferably outside friendship groups, ask the children to talk about their favourite book, their favourite food and their favourite day out. Emphasise how important it is for both partners to take turns to talk and listen. A key to relationship skill is being able to listen.

How do you know if someone is listening? Emphasise the four key points, that they:

- keep still
- keep quiet
- look at me
- remember what I say.

Reflection/plenary
Group the pairs into groups of six and ask them to introduce their partner to the group in turn, by saying one new thing they learnt about their partner.

Differentiation
- *Children needing more of a challenge* – could develop a word board, for example on what makes a good friend. Get children to suggest words as well as having some of your own, such as happy, funny, kind, nice, plays with me and shares.
- *Children with additional learning needs* – could use photo cards of different types of body language. (Photo cards can be bought commercially or you could make your own with the children posing for camera shots.) Different types of body language might include turning away, avoiding eye contact, crossing their arms, yawning, frowning or smiling. Discuss in small groups. Ask, 'Does this person look like a good friend?'

What if …
Children start arguing about an incident that happened at playtime?
Remind them of the working agreement and suggest that they talk about how to make things better at the end of the lesson. In doing so, remind the children to use the listening skills they have practised in the lesson. You may need to do more work about friendship and peaceful problem solving with the whole class in response to the issue.

Families of all kinds (Key Stage 1)

By the end of this lesson the children will identify and respect similarities and differences between families. and will know and understand why families are special for caring and sharing.

Learning outcomes
- I can tell you how my family is the same and different to my friends'.
- I can describe a number of different family situations.
- I can identify special people in my life.

Working agreement
Remind the children of the working agreement and explain that today we are going to talk about families. Explain that families are usually places of love and caring, but sometimes things can go wrong in families. Remind children of where they can go to talk to someone about their family if they need to. Emphasise that we are all special and should listen to each other.

Resources needed
Whiteboard or flip chart.

Opening activity: Hoops
Set out hoops across the floor labelled 0, 1, 2, 3, 4, 5+. Call out 'How many pets in your house?', 'How many people live in your house?', 'How many males?', 'How many females?', 'How many brothers and sisters (counting step and half brothers and sisters)'? and so on. Pupils move to the correct hoop.

Reflect that the game has showed how we all have very different families. Suggest this is something we should be proud of as it makes us and our family special – no two families are the same and all families are different.

Explain that pupils are going to look at some families and talk about why they are special.

Main activity: Family pictures
Organise a collection of images of different families. Try to ensure a range of families are shown, including families with same-sex parents/carers, multicultural families, single parent and so forth. Set images out on tables around the classroom before the lesson.

In small groups of three or four, pupils investigate the pictures and discuss the situation of each family and consider the following questions:

- Who is in the family? How many people?
- How do you know it is a family?
- What makes the family special?

Gather all groups back together and ask each group to present the family they have studied to the whole class. Repeat the questions above. Then ask children to reflect on their own families and to draw a picture to show their family. Allow time for them to draw. Pupils are allowed to opt out of the activity for whatever reason. If so, pupils can draw a family based on any of the pictures that have been discussed. Be sensitive to looked after children

Reflection/plenary

Put all the pictures on the wall and ask the children to walk around looking at other people's pictures. Ask them how many different types of family do we have in our class?

Differentiation

- *Children needing more of a challenge* – could write words to describe their family to go with their picture.
- *Children with additional learning needs* – could be supported to think about their family and can choose how to present their family.

What if …

Parents/carers complain about the range of families being discussed including families with lesbian and gay parents/carers? It would be good practice for parents/carers to be informed of the SRE programme and to know beforehand that throughout the curriculum a variety of family types will be acknowledged and that this supports the school's equalities duty to foster good relations. Ensure that a wide range of families from diverse backgrounds in the school community are acknowledged through the lesson, resources used, posters and so on. Parents/carers who complain can be reminded of the diverse society in which we live and the importance of children feeling that their family is valued alongside others. Ensure that parents/carers are aware of the range of work the school does to promote equalities and diversity.

Similarities and differences (Key Stage 2)

By the end of this lesson pupils will be able to respect other people's viewpoints and beliefs, see things from other people's viewpoints, have considered why being different can provoke bullying and why this is unacceptable, and express opinions, for example about relationships and bullying.

Learning outcomes
- I can listen well to others even when I disagree with what they are saying.
- I can tell you what bullying is.
- I understand that there are differences between people and I understand that these differences can enrich our lives.
- I understand how rumour-spreading and name-calling can be bullying behaviours.
- I can recognise what it feels like to feel different.
- I can explore and recognise stereotyping and prejudice.
- I know that name-calling is wrong and that it can be hurtful.

Working agreement
Remind the children about the working agreement and emphasise the importance of treating each other with respect.

Resources needed
- Cards with familiar pairs of words divided between them – for example, Marks/Spencer.
- Statements on cards for values continuum.

Opening activity: Pairs and fours
To form random pairs, have enough cards with familiar couples of words divided between them, such as Marks/Spencer, fish/chips, right/left, Harry/Potter. Put them all in a box or hat, mix well and ask the pupils to pick one out and then find their other half.

In these pairs, ask them to find two things they have in common and two things that are different. Put pairs into groups of four, and ask groups to find one thing they all have in common. Go round the class and ask each group to share the most unusual thing they have in common.

Discuss what's good about being similar and what's good about being different. Emphasise that we are all unique and how we should all be proud of our particular differences. Discuss whether the characteristics they have chosen are things you can choose or whether they are givens. Examples could include hair colour, skin colour, football team and favourite food.

Main activity: Values continuum
Start by explaining that we can also have different opinions and beliefs from each other. Explain the idea of a values continuum – a line that represents how strongly you agree with something from 'strongly agree' to 'strongly disagree'. You can do this as a physical activity, using an imaginary line across the classroom along which children stand according to their views about a series of statements (see examples of statements below). Alternatively, you can get children to work in groups using statements on cards and a line on a sheet of paper to indicate their views.

Main activity: Example statements
You will need to adapt these to reflect the interests of your class or to reflect some of the tensions that may exist in the class between different groups.

- School holidays are boring.
- You shouldn't lend your things to a friend.
- You should always do what your parents/carers tell you to do.
- Being a vegetarian is stupid.
- Children should give half their pocket money to charity.
- Name-calling is only teasing and is not meant to be hurtful.
- If you are in a hurry it is alright to run across the road/down the corridor.

Read the statements out and ask children to indicate whether they agree or disagree. Ask one child to explain their views, and then ask for someone who has a different opinion to explain their views. Compliment the class on how well they listened to each other.

Afterwards, discuss what it felt like when someone had a very different opinion from others. Ask them: 'Does it mean you are wrong?' Explain that lots of people have lots of different ideas and we can disagree with their ideas without disliking them or being horrible to them. Ask: 'How can we show that we respect each other's views even if we disagree with them?' (Answers are likely to include: listening, asking questions, and politely saying you don't agree.)

Ask: 'What happens when people don't respect each other's views and don't respect others' differences?' (Expect the answers: teasing, bullying, fighting, even wars.) Explain about discrimination and bullying being based on people not liking others being different and treating them differently. Remind children of the work that has previously been done on bullying and what to do if they or someone else is being bullied.

Reflection/plenary
Go round the class asking children to complete the sentence, 'It's good to be friends with people who are different from you because …'

Differentiation

- *Children needing more of a challenge* – could hold a formal debate about a given topic, with speakers on each side of the argument, and then take a vote at the end.
- *Children with additional learning needs* – could work with puppets to make up small plays or sketches about what happens when people disagree with each other and how they can still get on with each other.

What if ...

Someone says something about another child or adult that is clearly offensive and is related to difference (such as skin colour, sexual orientation or size)? You will need to challenge the comment using the working agreement and referring to the values of the school. You might want to ask the class: 'How would you feel if someone said something nasty about you because of a way that you're different to them?'

Gender roles and stereotyping (Key Stage 2)

By the end of this lesson, pupils will be able to recognise and challenge gender stereotypes, have considered why being different can provoke bullying and why this is unacceptable, and understand how the media impact on forming attitudes.

Learning outcomes
- I can discuss gender stereotypes.
- I can question and challenge assumptions based on stereotyping.
- I can explore and recognise stereotyping and prejudice.
- I know that the diversity of lifestyle choices enriches our society.
- I try to recognise when I, or other people, are prejudging people, and I make an effort to overcome my own assumptions.

Working agreement
Remind the children about the working agreement and emphasise the importance of treating each other with respect.

Resources needed
- Picture, model or toy of an alien
- Picture of a baby
- Magazine pictures of people
- Birthday cards, new baby cards and magazine pictures showing gender stereotyping.

Opening activity: Circle activity – pass the alien
Introduce a picture, model or soft toy representation of an alien (such as an inflatable model) and explain to the class that this creature comes from a planet where they don't have male and female so that he doesn't know how to tell the difference between girls and boys. Pass the alien around the circle asking the children to say what the differences are. Encourage each child to think of something new to add. Record their answers.

Ask them to imagine how the alien might reproduce.

Main activity: Gender timeline
Find a picture of a baby (try to find one that is fairly non-gender specific – so no blue or pink clothes!). Divide the class into two halves and tell one group that the baby is a girl and the other that it is a boy. Then subdivide the halves into smaller groups who will look at ages 5, 11, 16 and 25. Ask the children to draw and write about how they think the baby will grow up at ages 5, 11, 16 and 25 – its physical and emotional characteristics, toys it will play with, games it will play, clothes it will be wearing, hobbies it will have, jobs it might be doing and so on. Display the pictures on the classroom wall to form a timeline.

Then reveal that they were both looking at the same person and talk about the difference that being a boy or a girl makes in a person's life. Discuss whether there is only one way of behaving if you are a boy or a girl.

Be ready to challenge some of the assumptions by giving examples of non-stereotypical working roles: a man staying at home to look after children, a woman bus driver, a male nurse, a female firefighter and so on.

Discuss where we get our ideas about gender roles. Collect images from magazines, birthday cards and new baby cards, and discuss how men and women are portrayed (include non-stereotypical pictures too). Introduce and explain the word stereotype. What would happen if a boy or a girl wanted to do something that didn't fall within the stereotyped role? (Children may have seen the films *Billy Elliott* and *Bend it Like Beckham.*) What would family and friends say? How might the boy or girl feel? Talk about teasing and bullying because someone is different.

This could be a good opportunity to discuss issues around sexual orientation and homophobia, especially if terms like 'gay' are used if boys or girls do not comply with gender stereotypes. Give a simple explanation of what being 'gay' means and say why it is unacceptable to use it as an insult (refer to the feelings lesson in Theme 4). For example, in the same way as men and women can be attracted to and love each other, so can two men or two women. Remind the class that just as a man and woman can get married, two men or two women can form a civil partnership.

Reflection/plenary

Go round the class asking children to complete the sentence, 'Something that we've talked about today that has made me think is ...' *Or* make posters titled 'Girls will be girls' and 'Boys will be boys', which contradict all the easy stereotypes about genders.

Differentiation

- *Children needing more of a challenge* – could write a story in which traditional gender roles are reversed.
- *Children with additional learning needs* – could design a birthday card or new baby card that would be suitable for both sexes.

What if ...

- *Someone says, 'My Dad says that women should stay at home and look after the house'?* Open it up for class discussion. Ask: 'What do you think mums should do? Can dads stay at home and look after the house?' Acknowledge that individuals and families can have a range of views on men and women, but make sure that it is emphasised that everyone has the right to make their own decisions and that we all have the right to our own ideas. If necessary make it clear that in school boys and girls have equal rights to learn, to play sports and to be safe.
- *You have a child in the class with gender identity issues?* This makes it even more important that work takes place on gender stereotyping and that children are encouraged to view each other as individuals. (For more information visit the Gender Identity Research and Education Society (GIRES) at http://www.gires.org.uk.)

Trust and empathy (Key Stage 2)

By the end of this lesson pupils will be able to: recognise their changing emotions towards their families; see things from other people's viewpoints, for example their parents' and carers'; know and understand about the many relationships in which they are all involved; have considered the need for trust and love in established relationships; know and understand about, and accept, a wide range of different and diverse family arrangements, for example, married, divorced or separated parents, second marriages, fostering, extended families, same-sex parents, and three or more generations living together; and have considered how separation and loss affect people in the family.

Note that the learning objectives cover sufficient ground to allow for an extension lesson, particularly for the last two objectives.

Learning outcomes
- I can use peaceful problem solving to sort out difficulties.
- I am aware of different types of relationships, including marriage and civil partnership.
- I know that there are different types of family.
- I can understand how I might hurt others.
- I know how to see things from someone else's point of view.
- I know how most people feel when they lose something or someone they love.
- I know that my relationships are all different and that different ways of behaving are appropriate to different types of relationships.
- I know that family relationships can change.

Working agreement
Remind the children about the working agreement and emphasise the rule about treating each other with respect.

Resources needed
- Medium or large sheets of paper
- Pens and pencils
- Whiteboard or flip chart.

Opening activity: Trust trains
Ask pupils to line up behind one another in fours, with their hands on the shoulders of the person in front of them. They are a 'train' – the person at the back is the driver and the person at the front is the engine. To start the train, the driver makes two squeezes on the person in front's shoulders. They pass the squeeze forward until it reaches the engine, who moves the train forward until they receive another instruction. To stop the train = one squeeze; to turn right = squeeze the right shoulder; to turn left = squeeze the left shoulder. The engine should keep repeating an action until they receive another squeeze. The aim is for the driver to drive the train around the room without any train crashes. After a few minutes the engine goes to the

back of the line and becomes the new driver, and a new engine takes over. Repeat this until everyone has had a go. Encourage the children to go a little faster as they become more confident.

Ask how it felt to be a driver and an engine. Discuss the need to trust other people at times.

Main activity: Extended role play
This is whole group role play for whole classes. The scenario (loss and change/family) is that Jo is 10 years old. She has become very quiet over the past few weeks, having been a very bright and interested member of the class. You approach Jo one lunchtime and ask her if everything is alright as she seems a bit sad. She bursts into tears and starts to tell you …

1. What might be happening to Jo?
Ask the class to brainstorm ideas. This might bring up unhappiness at home and the lesson will then focus on this issue for the purpose of the exercise: Jo's mum and dad are going to get divorced, and the dad is going to live with her friend's mother. (An alternative scenario might be that Jo is being bullied because she lives with her mother and her mother's female civil partner or that Jo is being bullied because someone is saying that her uncle has AIDS – see Theme 5 lesson: Keeping clean and healthy during puberty (Key Stage 2).)

2. Who might be involved with Jo or with this situation?
Ask the class and record their suggestions.

3. Create a character
Each person chooses one of the characters, who they are going to develop further. On a slip of paper, ask them to write down:

- their person's name and age
- where they live in relation to Jo
- how they know what has happened
- how they feel about it.

4. Circle of relationships
With the whole group in a circle, the teachers asks questions of about six people. Each person should answer as if they were their character. Questions: As above, with some questions exploring the situation – for example, 'What's your name?', 'How do you know Jo?' and 'What do you think has happened?'

5. Hot seating
Organise the pupils into groups of three. Each person has about two minutes being asked by the other two in the group about the situation. The pupil in the 'hot seat' answers in role. Questions: 'How do you feel?', 'How do you think Jo/e feels?', 'How do the others in the situation feel?' and 'What might happen next?' (worst outcome/best outcome).

6. De-role
In same threes, take turns to say who you really are and what you like doing in your spare time.

7. Conscience corridor
Form two lines of children facing each other. Ask for a volunteer to stand in for Jo and to walk down the line as each pupil says a word or phrase that depicts what Jo might be feeling or thinking, with the line on the left saying what Jo might be thinking and the line on the right saying what Jo might be feeling. Ask the volunteer what they heard. Repeat this for someone else who has a key role in the situation – for example, Jo's mother (or the bully), reversing the thoughts and feelings lines.

Reflection/plenary
Ask the pupils how it felt to see a situation from someone else's point of view. What did they learn? How could the people in Jo's class help her? Who else could help?

Differentiation
- *Children needing more of a challenge* – could write a short play based on one of the scenarios discussed.
- *Children with additional learning needs* – could use a digital camera and create a storyboard on one of the scenarios.

What if ...
There is a child in the class who has two mothers? (She calls both of them Mum, but you overhear a child saying 'But you can't have two mums …')
As a core part of sex and relationships education and the classroom environment generally, teachers do need to make the class aware that single-sex partnerships are very much part of the range of family types. If this work has been going on you can remind both children that in the class we respect all different family types and it is possible to have two mums, two dads and so on. You may want to follow up with the child and her mums concerning whether there are any other issues emerging in school and how to can best support them.

What is a friend? (Key Stage 2)

By the end of this lesson pupils will have reflected on their friendships, who they choose to be friends with and what makes people best friends. There is also an opportunity to discuss why some people don't have best friends, friendships on the internet, same gender friendships and homophobia.

Learning outcomes
- I understand why friendship is important.
- I know that there are different kinds of friends and what I look for in a best friend.
- I know that people have different numbers of friends but what is important is what friends do for each other.

Working agreement
Remind the children about the working agreement and emphasise that we should not make personal remarks about others.

Resources needed
Whiteboard or flip chart.

Opening activity: Double circles
Ask people to join up in pairs and then form two circles, with one person in the inner circle and their partner facing them in the outer circle. Read out an unfinished sentence related to friendship and ask the pairs to complete it in turn. Then ask the people on the outside to move one place to their left to stand opposite a new partner. Read out a new sentence to complete. Sentences could include:

- I like people who …
- When I am left out …
- A funny thing (or scary thing) that happened to me and my friend …
- Something I enjoy doing with my friend …
- When I meet someone new …
- I dislike people who …
- People like me because …
- A best friend is …

When all the sentences have been read out, ask the class what are their thoughts about friends and friendship.

Main activity: Friendship circles
Demonstrate friendship circles on a flip chart, by drawing two circles and placing two or three of your own friends on it, closer friends in the inner circle and others in the outer circle. Ask children, individually, to list their friends (by initials if they prefer), and then to draw their own friendship circles. When they have done this, ask them to join up with someone else and to talk about what they have realised about their own pattern of friendship. They do not have to show their circles if they do not want to.

Review in the whole group by asking:

- Does everyone have the same number of friends?
- What if you have lots of friends/fewer friends?
- Why did you put some friends in the inner circle and others in the outer one?
- What is a best friend?
- Are all your friends other children?
- What about Facebook friends?
- Do you have close friends of the same or different gender?
- If you have a friend of the same gender will people call you a lesbian or gay?
- Does everyone have the same pattern of friendship?
- Is your current pattern fixed or will it change?

Reflection/plenary

In a circle complete the sentences: 'What I like most about my friend …' and 'What my friend likes most about me …'

Differentiation

- *Children needing more of a challenge* – could list the times when friendships change, e.g. moving to a new school and think of ways to make new friends.
- *Children with additional learning needs* – with a teaching assistant spend more time thinking about what a friend is, listing the qualities of a friend.

Follow-up

Carry out a class auction to identify the most important qualities in a friend. In groups, brainstorm all the things that are important in a friend and prioritise three. Write the three top qualities from each group on the flip chart, eliminating duplicates. Ask each group to put the list of qualities on the flip chart in order of importance. Give each group 10 tokens with which to bid for their top qualities in the auction. When all the qualities have been bought, ask the groups to review their success and discuss what most people think are important for friendships.

What if …

There is a child in the class who has or says they have no friends? As the children complete the circles, check for anyone who is not filling in the circles. You can suggest some people who they might include from your own observations, and ask about friends out of school, pets and other people who are important to them. Stress it doesn't matter if they only put a very few names on their circles.

Friendship problems (Key Stage 2)

By the end of this lesson pupils will have considered the main sources of friendship breakdown amongst their friends, how it makes them feel and how situations can escalate into bigger rows. They will learn how to communicate their feelings to another person in a non-aggressive manner, using an 'I' statement that doesn't blame or label them, instead focusing on their behaviour and its effects.

Learning outcomes
- I recognise the things that cause friendships to break down and how it makes people feel.
- I can tell someone I have fallen out with how I feel about what they have done without making the situation worse.
- I know that it is important not to bottle up bad feelings but find a way of expressing them constructively.

Working agreement
Remind the children about the working agreement and emphasise that we should not make personal remarks about others.

Resources needed
- Whiteboard or flip chart
- Separate pictures of two children
- Four large labels: A lot, Sometimes, Seldom, Never
- A list of things we might say in an argument with a friend.

Opening activity: Four corners
Show a picture of two children who have stopped being friends. Ask the class what might have happened?

Clear a space in the classroom and place four large labels – A lot, Sometimes, Seldom, Never – one in each of the four corners of the room. With the children standing in the central space, call out a cause of a friendship breakdown – for example, talking about you behind your back – and ask the class to move to the corner that matches how often they think this happens amongst their friends. When they have moved, ask for a few comments on how it might feel. Repeat with other causes, such as not sharing, leaving someone out, taking things without asking, telling tales, bullying, name-calling, going off with someone else and breaking promises. Each time, ask how it might make you feel.

Main activity: Making 'I' statements
One way of coping with these feelings is to be able to tell the other person how what they have done is making you feel. Take a situation, such as someone borrows your best pen and loses it. What do you feel like saying? Demonstrate – for example, 'You're useless'; 'Keep your hands off my things!' Consider how will the other person react – for instance, 'I don't care', 'The pen was rubbish.' What is the likely

outcome? Animosity; telling tales to the teacher. Another way is to use an 'I' statement. Demonstrate the formula:

- when you (what the other person did) for example when you lost my pen
- I felt (the feeling you experienced) e.g. I felt unhappy
- because (the effect on you or others) for example because my Dad gave it to me and he'll be cross it's lost.

What might the other person say to you now? Emphasise that an 'I' statement doesn't blame the other person but focuses on the consequences of their behaviour.

Give the pupils, in pairs or threes, a short list of things that we might say in an argument with a friend. Ask them to rewrite what they might say using the 'I' statement formula. Hear their responses and ask the class to check Are they using the formula? What might the other person say?

Reflection/plenary

In a circle complete the sentence: 'I'll try out an "I" statement next time someone …'

Differentiation

- *Children needing more of a challenge* – could develop more scenarios on a storyboard.
- *Children with additional learning needs* – with a teaching assistant explore the main activity using two puppets to demonstrate the formula.

Follow-up

1. *A new class member.* Show a picture of a child the same age as the class and ask them to imagine that this child is going to join the class tomorrow. How do they think that this child will be feeling today? In small groups, ask the children to think of all the ways they could be friendly towards them.
2. *Problem solving.* Introduce a problem-solving model – that is, looking at the problem from different points of view, thinking of a range of solutions, evaluating the potential outcomes of each solution and choosing the best solution. Give pupils opportunities to apply the problem-solving process to a range of problems in relationships.

What if …

There is a conflict within the class. It is important to use distancing techniques throughout this lesson. During the lesson stress the importance of resolving problems peacefully. If an argument arises within the class refer to the ground rules.

Sample assessment activities

Learning outcome	Assessment activity
I understand that boys and girls can like both the same and different things and that this is alright.	Children can be challenged to design some non-gender specific lunchboxes. These can then be assessed to show an understanding of how to avoid gender stereotypes. Record which pupils have met the learning outcome, are working towards or beyond it, or ascertain what follow-up work is needed.
I can tell you how my family is the same and different to my friends'.	The teaching assistant works with individuals (or a sample of the class representing different abilities) and asks them to explain the similarities and differences between their family and other families they have learnt about. Pupils can be assessed to be working at, towards or beyond the learning outcome. Observe the activities closely and reflect on how the children responded. Decide whether they need further work on this topic.
I can question and challenge assumptions based on stereotyping.	Give children a 'problem page' and ask them to respond to the writer orally or in writing to make them feel better. Use the responses from a sample of children to judge progress made in children's ability to challenge stereotypes and prejudice. For example: 'Hi, my name is Jane and every Saturday I play football in the park with my Dad. Some kids from school saw me and said that "girls are rubbish at football". It made me feel really embarrassed and I am not sure if I should play anymore. I love football. What should I do?'

Learning outcome	Assessment activity

I can listen well to others even when I disagree with what they are saying.	Ask children to self-assess themselves at the end of the lesson using the following statements. In today's lesson:
	
	• I listened well in paired discussion.
	  Yes / No / Some of the time
	• I listened well to the teacher.
	  Yes / No / Some of the time
	• I listened well when my friends were talking.
	  Yes / No / Some of the time
	• I listened well to others even when I disagreed with what they were saying.
	  Yes / No / Some of the time
	• I was able to express my own opinion, even when it was different to others in the class.
	  Yes / No / Some of the time
	
	Children could then set themselves a target. The self-assessments could then be collected in and added to other assessments to see how well children are working towards the end of the Key Stage statement or other benchmark of progress. Take a sample to verify, or look at other assessments.

I recognise the things that cause friendships to break down and how it makes people feel, and I can tell someone I have fallen out with what they have done without making the situation worse.	Storyboard: Provide blank storyboards/ cartoon strips and ask the children to illustrate what would happen with two characters after one breaks the other's favourite pencil. How would it be resolved peacefully? The storyboards can then be teacher- or peer-assessed.

Theme 4: Feelings and attitudes

Introduction

Feelings

Feelings can be overwhelming at any age. Even knowing what it is we're feeling and then knowing how to behave appropriately is difficult for many adults. No wonder we often deny their importance and adopt the 'ostrich position'. So showing children that feelings have names, that we all have them and that they can be coped with – especially the difficult ones like anger and sadness – needs to be a vital part of anyone's emotional and social development.

Primary schools are places where children can learn that feelings are normal and can be managed – by listening to stories, doing activities where they can identify different feelings and by practising 'pretend' social situations. They will also see adults and hopefully their peers expressing and dealing with feelings in appropriate ways. Using children's literature is also a good way to focus on feelings in different situations.

Loss and bereavement can be particularly difficult, although not uncommon, situations for schools to deal with and teach about, involving as they do acknowledging feelings, being able to talk, being able to listen and being aware of sources of help. For more information on bereavement and children visit www.childhoodbereavement.org.uk

Attitudes

Exploration of attitudes and values is of equal importance to work on developing knowledge and skills. Living in a multicultural and multifaith society, we need to encourage children to understand other cultures and religions, and how attitudes and values relating to the family and sexual matters are similar or different to our own. This principle should be applied throughout the SRE programme, with links to the RE curriculum. Involving faith communities in the development of effective SRE is something that primary schools are well placed to do, because they often have good relations with parents/carers and encourage them to come into school as much as possible (SEF 2004).

Work on gender and gender stereotyping have already been examined, but it is also important that pupils are provided with opportunities to explore their attitudes to themselves and to the world around them. In particular, schools will want to focus on providing opportunities for pupils to explore attitudes and values that are manifested through the media and how these can be challenged.

Choices and consequences

SRE provides much information for children about safe and healthy behaviour. In order to be able to put this knowledge into practice, children need to have opportunities to practise making choices and decisions. The skills of decision making involve being able to weigh up information, consider and resist pressures; being aware of the consequences of one's actions; as well as having the confidence and assertiveness to put the decisions into action. There are many good PSHE education and SRE resources that give children opportunities to consider a wide range of situations in which different choices can be made. Role play, drama, case studies and 'problem page' answers can all be used effectively in the primary classroom.

Key questions on 'Feelings and attitudes'

Years 1 and 2
- How can we tell when someone is happy/sad and so on?
- What effect can strong feelings have on our bodies?
- Who can I tell if I am feeling unhappy or worried?

Years 3 and 4
- What makes me feel good?
- What makes me feel bad?
- How do I know how other people are feeling?
- Why are my feelings changing as I get older?
- How do I feel about growing up and changing?
- How can I cope with strong feelings?

Years 5 and 6
- What kinds of feelings come with puberty?
- What are sexual feelings?
- What are wet dreams?
- What is masturbation? Is it normal?
- How can I cope with these different feelings and mood swings?
- How can I say 'no' to someone without hurting their feelings?
- What should I do if my family or friends don't see things the way I do?
- What do families from other cultures and religions think about growing up?
- Can I believe everything I see on the TV about perfect bodies, relationships, and girls and boys?

Feelings (Key Stage 1)

By the end of this lesson the children will be able to recognise and name their feelings, share their feelings with others and think about how feelings affect them.

Learning outcomes
- I can identify a range of feelings, for example happy, sad and angry.
- I can describe what an emotion makes me feel like in my body.

Working agreement
Remind the children about the working agreement and emphasise the importance of listening to others.

Resources needed
- Noisy musical shaker
- Whiteboard or flip chart
- Soft toy or puppet.

Opening activity: Silent rattle
Invite the children to form a circle, and then pass a tambourine, maracas or set of bells around the class asking the children to make as little noise as possible. At the end of the round, ask them how they felt as the instrument was passed around the circle. You can write all the feelings on a whiteboard or flip chart.

To build up 'feelings vocabulary' introduce the children to the idea of a feelings board, which is when you record, on the whiteboard or flip chart, the children's feelings at different times throughout the day or week. Use a different coloured pen each time you add words. At the end of the day or week, discuss with the class how our feelings change and what makes them change.

Main activity: Soft toy
Discuss three feelings including happy and sad, picking one other from the words in the silent rattle activity (above), such as nervous, scared or excited. Using a soft toy or puppet, discuss the feelings word and ask the children to describe what could making him or her feel like that. (For example: sad – 'I think Caitlin is feeling sad because her mum has gone to work.') Continue by asking children what makes them feel like that.

Reflection/plenary
In a circle, the teacher says 'Stand up and change places if you feel …':

- happy when someone smiles at you
- happy when a friend plays with you
- sad when you fall out with a friend
- sad when you lose something

- excited when you have been promised a treat
- excited when you are going on holiday.

Follow-up activity

Look back at the feelings board (the Opening activity) and reflect on the range of feelings experienced during the day or week. Use feelings cards and just ask children to all show the feeling in their faces and bodies. Ideally, the work on feelings will be an ongoing part of other social and emotional health and well-being work and PSHE education programme, and will link to literacy by building up 'feelings' word banks and exploring the feelings of characters in stories.

Differentiation

- *Children needing more of a challenge* – could use word cards with 'feeling' words on and photo cards with facial expressions on to discuss a range of emotions (upset, angry, annoyed and so on). They could then make sentences starting 'I was annoyed in school when …' They could also choose a piece of music or paint an abstract picture depicting an emotion (such as angry, happy or sad).
- *Children with additional learning needs* – could concentrate on a few feelings such as happy, sad, angry or worried, then practise recognising the facial expressions for each of them. They could take digital photos and use them for a guessing game. Also, maybe make masks on a stick. Illustrate each feeling and make up a story with the children holding up the masks at appropriate places.

What if …

- *Children find it very hard to come up with words for feelings?* Plan in some more work for the class on this topic and look for additional resources within the SEAL materials.
- *Children make disclosures when we are talking about feelings such as scared?* Use the ground rules and distancing techniques to prevent disclosures during lesson time. When asking pupils to talk about feelings consider asking them for school examples. For example, 'I feel nervous in school when …' If a child does make a disclosure, thank them for their honesty and tell them you will talk with them about it later. If appropriate follow up within the school child protection procedures.

Managing our feelings (Key Stage 1)

By the end of this lesson the children will be aware that their feelings and actions have an impact on others and understand that they have some control over their actions.

Learning outcomes
- I can see when someone is feeling sad or hurt.
- I can do things that help others feel better.
- I know one thing I can do to calm myself down.

Working agreement
Remind the children about the working agreement and emphasise the rule about treating each other with respect.

Resources needed
- Puppets
- Whiteboard/flip chart.

Opening activity: Hello, how are you?
Start with everyone standing. One child crosses the circle to shake hands and ask another, 'How are you? The person answers by saying how they are feeling – 'I am feeling …' The child who asks the question sits down, and the child who answers the questions then crosses the circle. Continue until all are sitting. The teacher will need to model the process.

Main activity: Puppets
Use two puppets, A and B, to enact a scenario where A has been unkind to B – for example by not letting him or her join in a game. Get the children to think about how B is feeling. In pairs give the children a set of feeling cards. Ask the children to pick out a feeling card from a bank and hold it up. Look at range of feelings shown.

Ask them to tell A how he has made his friend feel and what they think he should do. A then tells the children (through you) that he didn't realise that he had hurt B so much. Ask two children to step into the characters' shoes (cut out feet for them to stand on) or pair up all children and have half A and half B. Ask the Bs to tell the As how they feel and then the As say sorry. Listen to some as a class and ask them what A can do to make it up to B.

Ask the children to think about a time when they felt upset. Ask them what would have made them feel better. Go back to puppet B and ask the pupils to suggest ways he could feel better.

Reflection/plenary
Go round the class asking children to complete the sentence, 'Next time I see someone who looks upset I will …'

Differentiation
* *Children needing more of a challenge* – could complete the following sentences to show the consequences of certain actions:

  * 'If someone pushes me I feel …'
  * 'If someone shouts at me I feel …'
  * 'If someone is rude at me I feel …'
  * 'If someone fights me I feel …'
  * 'If someone is kind to me I feel …'
  * 'If someone smiles at me I feel …'
  * 'If someone helps me I feel …'

* *Children with additional learning needs* – could do further role play work with the puppet, exploring similar situations to those described above.

What if …
Children suggest that puppet B should hit puppet A? Get the puppet to talk into your ear and tell the children that he said he has tried hitting back before but that it ended up in a fight and he got hurt so he doesn't think that's a good idea.

Identifying and expressing feelings (Key Stage 2)

By the end of this lesson pupils will show that they can recognise the signs that indicate how someone is feeling and identify the physical effects of strong feelings, as well as some ways to calm down. (This lesson links with the 'Friendship problems' lesson under 'Relationships' on page 106.)

Learning outcomes
- I can recognise when I am beginning to get upset or angry and have some ways to calm down.
- I can manage my feelings and can usually find a way to calm myself down when necessary.
- I understand why it is important to calm down before I am overwhelmed by feelings of anger.

Working agreement
Remind the children about the working agreement to ensure a safe environment in which to share feelings. Emphasise that it is alright to show your feelings, but that it is important to do this appropriately. Also emphasise the importance of privacy and not telling tales.

Resources needed
Paper or card and art materials.

Opening activity: Pass the mask
In a circle, the first person makes a funny face. The next person mirrors the funny face. This person then moves their hand down their face as if to remove the mask. They then make a different funny face, which is passed on to the next person, and so on until everyone in the circle has had a turn.

Main activity: Frozen images
As a whole class, brainstorm all the 'feelings' words everyone can think of. Ask them to choose six of the most common feelings.

Divide the children into six groups and get them to create a 'frozen image' relating to one of the feelings words. Other groups try to guess what feeling they are representing.

Ask the pupils to think about: how we know what someone is feeling (by their facial expression, the way they hold themselves); and how different feelings affect our bodies on the inside (butterflies in the tummy, heart beating faster, hot face, wobbly knees, feet made of stone, heart sinking, feeling like flying). The class could make a display to illustrate some of these.

Emphasise the importance of finding ways of managing strong feelings like anger. Show the class a picture of a child, Jo, looking angry and ask them to think about:

- what might have made Jo angry?
- how might Jo react? (shouting, hitting, damaging something, running away)
- what could Jo do to calm down? (breathe deeply, exercise, talk to someone, count backwards from 20 and so on).

In threes, ask the children to tell each other of one occasion when they felt angry or very upset. What did they do? How did they react? What helped them to calm down? Use feedback from the groups to create a class poster on ways to calm down.

Reflection/plenary
In a circle ask pupils to complete the sentence, 'To calm down when I feel angry I ...'

Follow-up activity
You may need to do some more work on managing strong emotions and coping strategies. You could create a feelings tree on which children hang different coloured leaves to show how they are feeling at different times in the day or week.

Differentiation
- Children needing more of a challenge – could create a 'feelings dictionary' using as many different words as possible for each feeling.
- Children with additional learning needs – could make a small 'feelings book' with one word or phrase per page, such as 'This person feels sad because ...', and a line drawing of a face. Children could also pair up with a 'feelings friend' who can note how they feel each day and talk to them about it.

What if ...
The children express feelings inappropriately? You may want to spend time talking about and exploring appropriate ways of expressing the negative ones such as anger. Some teachers have found that having a big floor cushion in another room that children can go and 'engage with' is a good idea. Also, talk with them about what can happen if you bottle things up.

What influences my choices? (Key Stage 2)

By the end of this lesson pupils will recognise that every day they are faced with making many choices and decisions. They will understand that their decisions are guided by their personal values and by external influences, and that sometimes these influences can have negative consequences.

Learning outcomes
- I recognise some things that are important to me and how they might affect my choices.
- I can identify people and other influences on my decision making and that some of these are helpful and others unhelpful or harmful.

Working agreement
Remind the children about the working agreement and emphasise the importance of listening to each other.

Resources needed
Large labels: A, B, C

Opening activity: Timeline
Ask for a volunteer to describe carefully everything they have done since they woke up this morning (or the teacher can describe this). The other children put up their hands to mark each choice the speaker presents; another pupil keeps a tally. How many choices has the speaker made so far today? Ask the speaker which were the easy choices and which did they have to think about.

As we grow up we have more opportunity to choose for ourselves. It helps to understand the things that guide our decisions, both inside us and outside.

Main activity: Shifting subgroups
Clear a space in the centre of the room and label three points, A, B and C. Ask the pupils to stand in the centre and tell them you are going to offer them three choices. They have to choose one of the options: 'Which of these would you choose to have? Move to the A, B or C label – A, sense of humour; B, good looks; C, high IQ.' When they pupils are grouped around A, B and C, ask them how their choice might affect their career decisions.

Repeat with the following choices: 'Which would you rather be? – A, Olympic competitor; B, prime minister; C, pop star. How might this choice affect how you decide to spend your leisure time?' Repeat with: 'What would you rather have? – A, lots of friends; B, lots of money; C, a big family. How might this choice affect who you make friends with?'

Ask the pupils to reflect on what they have learnt about themselves by making these choices. Different things are important to different people and these values do influence the choices and decisions we make.

Main activity: Influences spider diagram

Ask the children to think about all the people and things that are important to them, including family, carers, friends, school, famous people, TV programmes, social media, magazines they read and adverts they like. Ask them to draw a circle in the centre of a piece of paper and write 'Me' in it, then put people and things on a list around it, close to 'Me' if they are very important, further away if they are less important (with the teacher demonstrating on the flip chart). When they have finished their diagrams, ask them to pair up and discuss the following questions:

- Who or what has the most influence on you?
- How do these people/things influence you?
- Do you feel they bring out the best in you?
- Which people/things have the weakest influence on you? Why?
- Do any of these get you into trouble? How could you change this?
- Can you think of a recent decision you made that was influenced by (a) your family, (b) your friends, (c) the media, celebrities, advertising or social media sites?

Open up the discussion to the whole group, asking pupils for examples of when their decisions were influenced by different people or things. Has anyone ever made a bad decision as a result of one of these influences?

Reflection/plenary

Go round the class asking children to complete the sentence, 'When I am making a decision, one thing that is important to me is ...'

Differentiation

- *Children needing more of a challenge* – could draw up a table comparing the positive and negative influences of friends, family, media etc. on decisions that affect their health or could write a story about an imaginary character which illustrates these different influences.
- *Children with additional learning needs* – could choose the helpful and harmful influences from scenarios such as a friend offering you a cigarette or encouraging you to tell a teacher about a bullying incident, presented as pictures or cartoons.

Follow-up

Introduce stages of decision making and give pupils opportunities to apply a decision-making process to a range of scenarios.

You may wish to explore using the Philosophy for Children approach to thinking about choices (see the 'Resources' page at http://www.teachingthinking.net) and many Citizenship resources will include ideas for exploring moral dilemmas.

What if ...

- *Everyone wants to be a pop star or a millionaire?* Ask them to think about why so many people choose these options. Do they think that celebrity and money are the only worthwhile aspirations? Ask them to move to the other positions and think about what people might value and who make these different choices.
- *Pupils blame named persons for being a bad influence?* Remind them at the outset of the lesson that they should protect other people's privacy by avoiding use of names (see Working Agreement).

Sample assessment activities

Learning outcome	Assessment activity
I can identify the feelings of happy, sad and angry.	Give individual children (or a sample) a range of photo cards showing different scenarios, such as a seaside picture where a child has lost their parent/carer in the crowd or a picture of a child winning a teddy at the fair, and ask them to identify how these would make them feel. Note any children who find it hard to identify the feelings and plan follow-up work.
I know one thing I can do to calm myself down.	Listen carefully to children's responses to the closing activity and observe them at work and play over the coming weeks. Do any children need further support with managing strong emotions?
• I know some ways to calm myself down. • I can use my calming down strategies.	Ask pupils to write down the calming down strategies they like to use and then, over the week, keep a diary of when they have used these strategies. Collect these in and use them along with your own observations of children to identify whether they are working towards, at or beyond the level/end of Key Stage statement. Children who are struggling to manage their feelings appropriately could be referred into a small group for extra work.
I can identify people and other influences on my decision making and understand that some of these are helpful and others are unhelpful or harmful.	Using scenarios, ask pupils to create a role play in pairs or small groups illustrating choices with possible positive or negative outcomes, including scenarios illustrating them resisting pressure. For example, Ben and Dan steal a sweet from the corner shop. Ask what and who influences their decision to steal? Make a list of responses and circle the unhelpful influences.

Theme 5: Keeping safe and looking after myself

Introduction

Personal hygiene
Any teacher will tell you that, despite all the adverts on TV for soap, there are many children who have not been shown the basics of how to wash and be hygienic. Health professionals, too, know very well that ignorance of how infections are transmitted is often the contributing factor to a disease being spread. This issue becomes especially important as children get closer to puberty. Primary schools need to ensure that personal cleanliness and pastoral care are included in the curriculum. A school nurse can often be a valuable ally in the classroom. This work will also help prepare the children for more in-depth work in Key Stages 3 and 4 on HIV/AIDS and sexually transmitted infections.

Personal safety
Personal safety is a key whole-school issue and strategies and skills for children can be learnt via PSHE education. This work will include: recognising and identifying emotions such as feeling comfortable, uncomfortable, scared or unhappy; having a familiar vocabulary with which children can describe their bodies; being able to identify a number of adults to turn to when in need (particularly important when one of this number may have abused their trust); and learning assertiveness skills and knowing about privacy.

Given that children are more likely to be abused by someone known to them, it is important that this work does not focus on 'stranger danger'. Experience with children who have been asked to draw a stranger shows that 'stranger' is not a very meaningful concept for young children (they drew aliens and, in one case, an octopus!). A more useful approach might be to start with what makes children feel safe. Again, fiction can provide a safe way of providing opportunities to think about emotions and what to do if you feel unsafe.

Supporting children to develop protective skills
If we want to help children to develop protective skills, we need to ensure they can identify and deal with any situation in which they do not feel safe and encourages them to make their own decisions and take responsibility for these choices. The core principles for Protective Behaviours (adapted from Margetts and Lynch 2004) that underlie being safe are:

- 'We all have the right to feel safe all the time'
- 'There is nothing so awful (or too little) we can't talk about it with someone.'

The following are useful questions to explore with children:

- What is 'feeling safe'?
- How can we trust intuitive and physical feelings (early warning signs)?

- How do we think, feel and behave when we feel unsafe? (Our feelings are neither right nor wrong but our behaviour, on the other hand, is a choice with an effect.)
- What are our 'rights and responsibilities'? How can we respect both our own and others' rights (this includes, for instance, issues of coercion, bullying and abusive behaviour).
- Why do we take risks on purpose? Especially when it feels scary and yet we want the outcome, while at the same time remembering others' right to feel safe with us.
- What are the 'unwritten rules' that condition our thinking and behaviour, such as peer pressure?
- What are our 'support networks' and how to build, use and maintain them?

Once the core process has been taught, children are encouraged to use the ideas to anticipate possible challenges and to practise problem solving. This can be done in many creative ways: for example, through peer teaching, performance, creative writing, artwork, songs and discussion.

Key questions on 'Keeping safe and looking after myself'

Years 1 and 2
- Which parts of my body are private?
- When is it alright and when is it not alright to let someone touch me?
- How can I say 'no' if I don't want someone to touch me?
- Who should I tell if someone wants to touch my private parts?

Years 3 and 4
- What are good habits for looking after my growing body?
- What do I do if someone wants me to do something dangerous, wrong or that makes me feel uncomfortable?
- When is it good or bad to keep secrets?

Years 5 and 6
- How can I look after my body now I am going through puberty?
- How can girls manage periods (menstruation)?
- How can people get diseases from sex and can they be prevented?
- What is HIV, how do you get it and how can you protect yourself from it?

Keeping safe (Key Stage 1)

By the end of the lesson pupils will recognise safe and unsafe situations and recognise the physical warning signs of feeling unsafe. They will be able to suggest some ways that they can keep themselves safe, including identifying trusted adults who can help them.

Learning outcomes
- I can describe a situation where I would need adult help.
- I can understand simple rules for keeping myself safe.
- I can identify people who can keep me safe and how to ask for help from them.

Working agreement
Remind the children about the working agreement and remind them in particular that some things may be better talked about in private than with the whole class. Make sure they know when they can come and talk to you in private, although you may not be able to keep confidential everything that they may tell you.

Resources needed
- Puppet
- Large body outline.

Opening activity: Story
Using a puppet called Andy, the teacher tells a story about his day, including situations where Andy is safe and unsafe. Include some of the following: cutting bread with a sharp knife, dropping a ball in the road, holding mum's hand to cross the road, seeing older children arguing in the playground, teacher welcoming him with a smile, waiting for mum to meet him after school, a friend's uncle offering to give him a lift home and being tucked up in bed by his dad.

Pause after each situation and ask the children to call out if Andy is safe or unsafe. Make a list of the situations when someone might not feel safe.

Main activity: Body outline – warning signs
Use the unsafe situations listed in the previous activity and build on previous work on feelings. Using a large body outline, invite children to think about what happens to their bodies when they know they are in an unsafe situation. To help them, give them some scenarios (someone being unkind to them, getting lost, going somewhere or doing something they don't want to do) and draw on the physical signs of feeling unsafe (heart beating fast, wobbly knees, butterflies in the tummy, heavy feeling, hunched shoulders and such like). These are their 'let's get out of here' signs, a warning that they may be in an unsafe situation and need to do something to keep themselves safe. This is a good opportunity to use drama to look at body language and personal space.

Keeping ourselves safe: Remind the children of all the ways they said they were changing since they were babies. Add that one of the ways they are changing is that they are now getting old enough to help keep themselves safe. Get them to come up with a class list, or display, of all the ways they can do this. (For example: ask a grown-up, hold their hand, think before rushing off, handle scissors and knives carefully, listen to their warning signs and – the main rule (at this age) – tell a trusted adult if anything is making them feel unsafe.) Theme 6 'People who can help me' deals with identifying appropriate adults to talk to.

Reflection/plenary

In a circle, ask the children to complete the sentence, 'If I felt unsafe I could …' (with the teacher modelling by giving the first response). Pass a smile or hand squeeze round the circle.

Differentiation

- *Children needing more of a challenge* – could make a 'keeping safe' book listing dangerous activities and how to keep safe.
- *Children with additional learning needs* – could work with the learning assistant to create a group display showing ways to keep safe.

Note that the concept of 'safe' is difficult for some younger children to grasp. This needs to be kept in mind and reinforced at regular intervals.

Follow-up

Keeping safe with people. Create a collage to show all the people who can help keep us safe – for example families including pets, friends, grown-ups and people whose job it is to keep us safe. Add the captions 'Who can help me keep safe?' and 'What do they do to keep me safe?'

What if …

A child discloses that someone at home has made them feel unsafe? Gently follow up on the working agreement by saying that this is something the child could talk to you about in private after the lesson. Find a time to talk to them as soon as possible, praise them for being brave enough to tell you, do not promise confidentiality, and say you will try to get someone to help them. Follow the school's child protection procedures.

Setting personal boundaries (Key Stage 1)

By the end of this lesson pupils should be able to understand that there are different types of touch and understand the difference between safe, unsafe and unwanted touch.

Learning outcomes
- I know about parts of my body that are private and should not be touched without my permission.
- I can recognise how my behaviour affects other people.
- I understand the difference between right and wrong.

Working agreement
Remind pupils of the agreement and emphasise that it is important to listen to each other.

Resources needed
Girl and boy individual body outlines.

Opening activity: Brainstorm
Ask the children to call out different types of touches – for example, hitting, stroking and hugging. Make a list and ask the class which ones are nice touches and which ones are nasty touches. Sometimes touches that can be nice feel nasty when you don't want to be touched in that way, such as being hugged by someone you don't know well. Introduce the idea that you don't have to be touched if you don't want to – it's your body after all!

Main activity: Body outlines
Using the list, explain three kinds of touches:

1. *Safe touch:* These are touches that keep children safe and are good for them, and that make children feel cared for and important. Safe touches can include hugging, pats on the back and an arm around the shoulder. Safe touches can also include touches that might hurt, such as removing a splinter. Explain to children that when you remove a splinter you are doing so to keep them healthy, which makes it a safe touch.
2. *Unsafe touch:* These are touches that hurt children's bodies or feelings (for example, hitting, pushing, pinching and kicking). Teach children that these kinds of touches are not alright. Also teach children about another kind of unsafe touch: 'Another kind of unsafe touch is when a bigger person touches you on your private body parts and it is not to keep you clean or healthy. So we have a safety rule that it is never alright for any person to touch your private body parts except to keep you clean and healthy.'
3. *Unwanted touch:* These are touches that might be safe but that a child doesn't want from that person or at that moment. It is alright for a child to say 'no' to an unwanted touch, even if it is from a familiar person.

Using body outlines of a boy and girl, in small groups ask the children to draw someone giving them a safe touch, someone else giving them an unsafe touch and then colour in which parts of the body should not be touched unless you give permission.

Reflection/plenary

Help your children practise saying 'No' or 'Stop it, I don't like that' in a strong, yet polite voice. This will help children learn to show when their personal boundaries have been crossed.

Differentiation

- *Children needing more of a challenge* – could think about all the different people who touch them and who they touch. Do they always ask permission when they touch someone else?
- *Children with additional learning needs* – could use a puppet or toy to identify how different types of touches might make them feel and to tell the puppet what to say to unwanted or unsafe touches.

What if ...

A child discloses that a family member has been touching them? Gently follow up on the working agreement by saying that this is something the child could talk to you about in private after the lesson. Find a time to talk to them as soon as possible, praise them for being brave enough to tell you, do not promise confidentiality, and say you will try to get someone to help them. Follow the school's child protection procedures.

Keeping yourself clean and healthy (Key Stage 1)

By the end of this lesson the children will know and understand basic rules for keeping clean and healthy and understand that they have some control over the choices they make about looking after their bodies.

Learning outcomes
- I can describe and carry out basic hygiene routines, using soap, toothpaste and shampoo correctly.
- I can explain why it is important to keep clean.
- I can identify some things I eat and drink, and some activities I do that help to keep me healthy.
- I understand what it means to be healthy and know what healthy choices are.

Working agreement
Remind children about the working agreement and emphasise that it is alright to laugh at something funny but not at another person.

Resources needed
Objects for Kim's Game.

Opening activity: This is my ear
In a circle, one person points to one part of their body (for example, their foot) and says, 'This is my ear!' The person next to them points to their ear and says a different part of the body, such as 'This is my arm!' and so on round the circle.

Main activity: Kim's Game and mime
Put a number of objects related to keeping clean and healthy on a tray (soap, a toothbrush, toothpaste, apple, carrot, towel, tissue/hanky and so on). Remove one object at a time (under a cloth so the children can't see) and ask them to remember which object is missing. You could also include an 'odd one out' such as a sweet. At the end, ask the children if they can think what all the objects have in common.

Using the same objects, form small groups and give each group one of the objects. In turn, ask each group to mime the object being used; the class tries to guess what it is. Then discuss why this object is important to keep us clean and healthy.

Discuss other healthy choices like going to the doctor or dentist, exercise and so on. Talk about who is responsible for making healthy choices and how this changes as we grow up – mostly it's the adults that care for them, but now they are getting older they can decide too. Make a class list of healthy decisions they can make to keep themselves healthy and clean.

Reflection/plenary

Go round the class asking children to complete the sentence, 'One thing I'm going to do to keep myself clean and healthy is …'

Differentiation

- *Children needing more of a challenge* – could increase the number of objects or add unfamiliar items or give time limits in Kim's Game – or do all of these. Encourage them to think about the different ways things get into our bodies, such as: through our mouths (food, water, medicine); our noses (breathing air, germs) and so on.
- *Children with additional learning needs* – could reduce the number of objects in Kim's game. Or they could use the outline of the missing object (a visual clue) to assist them with matching and memory, and work in pairs.

What if …

There is a child in the class who is often dirty and smelly? Remind the class of the working agreement about treating each other kindly. The school should be contacting the parents or carers about this problem. Maybe the school nurse, learning mentor or home school liaison worker could help by talking to the child and their family. Some schools have a supply of spare clothes to lend out if necessary.

Keeping safe – understanding risk (Key Stage 2)

By the end of this lesson pupils will know and understand about keeping themselves safe when involved with risky activities, and understand when it is appropriate to take a risk and when to say no and seek help.

Learning outcomes
- I know how I can make things less risky and be responsible for myself.
- I can talk about ways of keeping myself safe.
- I can identify the different types of risks people take and can consider the outcomes of risk-taking.
- I can make a judgement about whether to take a risk.
- I can establish rules for keeping safe.

Working agreement
Remind the children about the working agreement and emphasise that, although we should not talk about personal issues with the whole class, it is alright to speak to you or another teacher in private. Remind children of the limits of adult confidentiality in the class.

Resources needed
- Sets of cards of risk situations
- Most risky/Least risky labels.

Opening activity: All change
This activity will help you establish what the children think a risk is. We tend to think of risks as something negative, but we take risks all the time. In a circle ask the pupils to stand up and change places if they have ever:

- told someone a secret
- eaten sweets
- crossed the road without looking
- swum in the sea.

Most children will have moved places by the end of the activity. Ask them, 'Does everyone take risks?' and 'Are all risks the same?'

Main activity: Risk continuum card sort
Write the following risk situations on sets of cards. Divide the class into small groups and give each group a set of risk cards. Give each small group two labels: 'Most risky' and 'Least risky'. Ask them to look at each of the situations and put them in order of how risky they are. The situations are:

- you get a lift home from school from a friend's mum
- you get a lift home from a stranger
- you smoke a cigarette
- you run across the road when the pedestrian crossing is red
- you find your mum's packet of pills on the coffee table

- an adult you don't know very well puts their arm around you
- you drink some of your parent's wine
- you climb to the top of a tree or climbing frame
- you see a group of children teasing another child
- you take some sweets from the local shop
- you ride a bicycle to school
- you ask someone to play with you
- you argue with your friend.

When the groups have completed the task, ask them to discuss which are the *most* risky (that is, those situations in which you will come to physical harm), what are the different kinds of risk (physical, emotional, legal) and can you make some activities safer (for example, learning to ride a bicycle and sticking to the rules for crossing the road).

Based on the discussion of the situations above, make a list of useful strategies for keeping safe. The list could include: tell a grown-up, think before you act, say no, don't be pressured, remember safety rules, and always 'tell' if you are worried or scared or just feel that something is not right.

Reflection/plenary
In a circle, ask the children to say one thing they have learnt today.

Differentiation
- *Children needing more of a challenge* – could make a poster with simple safety rules for nursery and Key Stage 1 children.
- *Children with additional learning needs* – could practise ways of saying no in different situations through role play.

Follow-up
ICT: invite the children, in groups, to use a digital camera to create a 'freeze frame' of some of the risk scenarios. The children can then paste these into PowerPoint presentations and label them with speech and thought bubbles and captions. Share age-appropriate ones in assembly as well as in Key Stage 1 classes.

What if …
You are asked or told by a pupil about something highly risky with which they, or another child (or even family member), is involved? Don't dismiss what they have said but gently follow up on the working agreement by saying that this is something the child could talk to you about in private after the lesson. You would need to use your professional judgement as to what to do. If it involved suspicion of abuse or other kind of criminal activity you would obviously report it to the headteacher and/or the child protection person and follow the school's child protection procedures. Find a time to talk to the child as soon as possible, do not promise confidentiality, and say you will try to get someone to help them. The teacher must provide consistent support during any referral or child protection procedure.

Some disclosures (such as evidence that children in the class are smoking) would need to be followed up in the classroom with a focus on the issue raised.

Asserting personal boundaries (Key Stage 2)

By the end of this lesson pupils should be able to say 'no' assertively. This lesson is linked to the lesson on 'Decision making' particularly the 'Who influences us' activity (see page 118). Theme 4 lesson: What influences my choices? **(Key Stage 2)**.

Learning outcomes
- I can distinguish passive, aggressive and assertive responses.
- I know how to say 'no' assertively.
- I understand the benefits of being assertive.

Working agreement
Remind pupils of the agreement and emphasise that it is important to listen to each other.

Resources needed
Scenarios for saying 'no'.

Opening activity: Saying 'no'
Standing in pairs, A and B, A will try to persuade B to do something they don't want to do but, As can only say 'yes' and Bs can only say 'no'. Encourage them to try out different ways of saying 'yes' and 'no'. Then swap round so that each pupil tries out both roles.

Main activity: Assertiveness trios
Emphasise that there are lots of different ways to say 'no', but you need to look as if you mean it. Ask the pupils to think about the opening activity – which ways of saying 'no' were most convincing? Shouting or looking away, fidgeting and mumbling are less convincing than keeping eye contact and saying no steadily and clearly. These are different ways to say 'stop' or 'no' – passively, aggressively or assertively. Ask children to volunteer to show how they said 'no' in these three different ways. Focus on the assertive response and ask the children to identify how to show you mean what you say – that is, to face the person and keep eye contact, speak clearly, keep calm, use 'I' statements and keep repeating your 'no'.

Prepare some scenarios in which a person would want to say 'no' assertively – for example, someone wants you to try a cigarette, someone wants you to play without asking parents' permission or someone wants to borrow your toy.

In groups of three, the pupils will practise saying 'no' assertively. Give the scenarios to the children and number the children 1, 2 and 3. Using the scenario, Number 1 makes the request to Number 2; Number 2 responds by saying 'no'. Number 3 observes how Number 2 responds assertively and gives them some feedback. Repeat the exercise twice more, with a new scenario each time and switching the roles round the trio so that all three pupils have a turn at saying 'no'.

Discuss what other situations children may be in when they may need to say 'no' assertively, such as peer pressure to do something risky.

Reflection/plenary
In a circle say how it felt to say 'no' assertively.

Follow-up
Peer pressure activity – scenarios where children have to be able to say 'no' to friends.

Differentiation
- *Children needing more of a challenge* – could make an illustrated leaflet or poster showing passive, aggressive and assertive responses.
- *Children with additional learning needs* – could think about situations when people ask them to do things they don't want to do and act out saying 'no' in different ways, perhaps using a puppet or toy.

What if …
A child discloses that a family member has been touching them inappropriately? Follow up on the working agreement by saying that this is something the child could talk to you about in private after the lesson. Find a time to talk to them as soon as possible, praise them for being brave enough to tell you, do not promise confidentiality, and say you will try to get someone to help them. Follow the school's child protection procedures.

Keeping clean and healthy during puberty (Key Stage 2)

By the end of the lesson pupils will know and understand that you have to take extra care with personal hygiene during puberty. Work on bacteria and viruses will need to be cross-referenced with any work in science.

Learning outcomes
- I know how I can care for my body and that I have to take responsibility for my own health.
- I know why washing is important.
- I know what I need to do to keep clean.
- I know how to keep myself clean and that certain parts of the body need careful washing during puberty.

Working agreement
Remind the children about the working agreement and emphasise that we should not make personal remarks about others.

Resources needed:
- Whiteboard or flip chart.
- Tray with objects relating to personal hygiene and something to cover them.
- Two large body outlines for the group work and individual small ones for the closing activity.

Opening activity: Kim's Game
Play this with a range of objects and products relating to personal hygiene, such as soap, tissues, toothbrush/paste, deodorant, sponge/flannel, towel, shampoo, nail brush, spot cream, razor and clean socks/pants, sanitary protection and washing powder. Put the objects on a tray. Remove one object at a time (under a cloth so the children can't see) and get them to remember which object is missing.

Discuss with the class why all these items are important as you get older and take more responsibility for looking after yourself. (Note: Your school nurse may be able to help you obtain free samples, for example of soap and toothpaste, for this lesson.)

Main activity: Body outline/hygiene diary
Discuss with the class the two main reasons for keeping clean: (a) to prevent body odour; and (b) so that we keep healthy and don't either spread or catch germs and infections.

Use two body outlines, either on the whiteboard or flip chart, to record all the children's ideas about how infections pass from one person to another. (Expect answers like: sneezing, putting dirty hands in our mouths, infections in the air getting in when we cut ourselves, breathing in germs and touching someone. Sex and sharing needles may also come up.)

In small groups, ask the pupils to discuss how we can protect ourselves and reduce the risk of infection: barrier (for example, putting a plaster on a cut) and avoiding contact (such as not drinking dirty water).

Remind children of the importance of washing their sexual body parts – particularly that girls should only wash with water and that boys with foreskins need reminding to pull these back to clean them. This discussion is a further opportunity to talk about these body parts as ones that others would need our permission to touch.

This exercise also provides an opportunity to introduce the topic of HIV and AIDS in the context of learning about the transmission of bacteria and viruses. Talk with the class about a serious infection they may have heard of called HIV. Explain how it is not like other infections you have talked about today because it is transmitted (passed) from one person to another by:

1. Their blood – getting from one person's bloodstream to another person's bloodstream.
2. From sexual intercourse – from one person's sexual organs to another's.
3. From mother to baby.

It leads to a condition they may also have heard of called AIDS. In some countries, thousands of people have HIV and there is no cure. To prevent it, people need to avoid coming into close contact with someone else's blood. With older children explain that the HIV virus can be found in other body fluids including semen and vaginal fluid. If the class already know about condoms, you can explain that they can be used to prevent passing on HIV. Tell children that other diseases can also be passed on through the blood (and other body fluids) and repeat the key message that we should avoid touching each other's blood and refer to the use of gloves during first aid. (See the case study at page 96 in Blake and Power 2003.) Emphasise that you can't tell by looking at someone that they have HIV.

To give the class an opportunity to empathise with someone who has the condition try out the whole-class role play in the 'Trust and empathy' lesson under Theme 3, Relationships (page 101). The scenario: Jo is being bullied because someone is saying that her uncle has AIDS.

Hygiene diary: Give children a template for a day diary with key times of day marked (for example, on waking, after breakfast, lunchtimes and before bed) and ask them to devise symbols to mark on hygiene routines for each time, and add in top tips for boys/girls.

Reflection/plenary

Using the information they have learnt, ask groups to come up with three questions they could use to quiz the other groups on knowledge acquired.

Differentiation

- *Children needing more of a challenge* – could find out about how important clean water is and how unclean water affects children all over the world, or could find out about how HIV affects children all over the world (see UNICEF and UNAIDS websites for more information).
- *Children with additional learning needs* – could draw and label items to put in a suitcase to keep clean and safe when packing to go on holiday.

Follow-up

For more in-depth discussion on HIV you may want to give an HIV quiz.

What if ...

- *There is a child being picked on by others because their personal hygiene is not what it should be?* You or the school nurse may choose to talk to the parent/carer about reasons for this happening and the resulting problems for the child. Remind the class of the working agreement about treating each other kindly. Maybe the school nurse, learning mentor or home school liaison worker could help.
- *There is an HIV positive child in the class?* In many cases the teacher and the school will not know if there are any children in school who are HIV positive or have family members who are. This lesson will need to be delivered sensitively so that it is supportive to those who have a direct experience of HIV. If stigmatising or prejudiced views of those with HIV emerge during this lesson these will need to be challenged and the issue will need to be followed up in the next lesson. If a teacher does know of an HIV positive child it will be important to inform them (and potentially their parents/carers) of the lesson and provide a right to pass or a right to say what they think are the important messages about HIV for children their age.

Sample assessment activities

Learning outcome	Assessment activity
I know about parts of my body that are private and should not be touched without my permission.	Give out some body outlines and ask children to draw and write the private parts of the body that should not be touched without their permission. Ask children to draw and write what they would do if they felt unsafe at any time or someone touched them in a way they did not like. Collect these in and assess them against the learning outcomes identified and the levels being worked towards.
I can understand simple rules for keeping myself safe.	Give children a scenario of a possible risk situation and ask them to explain how they would manage this. Children could draw and write their responses or tell them to you or a teaching assistant. Based on their responses, assess children's skills for keeping safe.

Learning outcome	Assessment activity
I know how to keep myself and my clothes clean and that certain parts of the body need careful washing during puberty.	Give children a 'problem page' letter from a boy or girl their age concerned about their friend who smells bad. Ask children to write a response to this letter detailing what information their friend might need, what products they should use and where they could go for extra help. Collect these in and assess against the learning outcomes.
I understand what healthy choices are.	Use two line-drawings of a child's body – one with a happy face and one with a sad face – and write over the top the titles 'Things that help keep me clean and healthy' and 'Things that make us less healthy'. Note: Avoid talking in terms of good and bad because, especially in the case of food, there are no bad foods, just foods that may not be healthy if we eat them every day. Give the children lists or pictures cut from magazines – which could include soap, toothpaste, shampoo, pop, sweets, fruit, water, cigarettes, burgers, chips, and vegetables – and ask them to place them on the appropriate line-drawings. Assess children's understanding of healthy choices following the activity.

Theme 6: People who can help me

Introduction

Finding someone to talk to is often the next stage on from acknowledging feelings. Helping children to have the confidence to express themselves clearly is at the heart of good primary practice anyway but, in SRE, schools can also ensure that children know who the best sources of help may be if they are worried or have a problem. Children can be encouraged and supported to talk to their parents/carers about growing up and relationships, and some schools provide support to parents/carers to facilitate this process.

Discussions in class can help children identify who 'people they trust' may be; and give extra information about local services (including the school nurse), dependable helplines (for example, the phone number for ChildLine, 0800 1111) and websites. Some schools also operate 'buddy schemes' where older pupils are trained to be 'listening ears' for younger children.

Key questions on 'People who can help me'

Years 1 and 2
- Who can I ask if I need to know something?
- Who can I go to if I am worried about something?

Years 3 and 4
- Who can I talk to if I feel anxious or unhappy?
- Where can I find information about growing up?

Years 5 and 6
- Who can I talk to if I want help or advice?
- Where can I find information about puberty and sex?
- How can I find reliable information about these things safely on the internet?

Someone to talk to (Key Stage 1)

By the end of this lesson the children will be able to identify and talk with someone they trust.

Learning outcomes
- I can describe a situation where I would need adult help.
- I can identify 'safe' people in my community who I can ask for help.
- I know who can help me best when something is wrong – for example, the dentist for toothache.

Working agreement
Remind children about the working agreement and emphasise that it's alright to ask for help.

Resources needed
- Cushions or other soft objects for obstacles
- Puppet
- Coloured paper, pens/crayons, scissors.

Opening activity: Trust game
Ask the children to form a circle, and then put 'obstacles' such as cushions in the middle. Blindfold one of the children and ask another to lead them across the circle around the obstacles. Repeat with other children taking the roles of leader and blindfolded follower. Discuss how it feels to need help and to have someone help you. Talk about how you need to be able to trust them.

Main activity: Puppet circle activity
In a circle, the teacher holds a puppet or a teddy bear and says that they want to tell you something that has been worrying them but that they are scared and do not quite know how to say it. Ask the children to give the puppet encouragement to tell you.

The puppet might tell you, for example:

- that someone has been bullying them
- that they are worried about their sister/brother
- that they don't understand their maths
- that they are worried they've lost their reading book.

The teacher hands the puppet to a child in the circle and asks them to say what they think the puppet is worried might happen. Repeat by asking the child to hand the puppet to another child across the circle and giving another reason to respond to. Repeat again until several children have contributed.

Ask the children to think about what they would do if the puppet asked them for help. Talk about the people children could talk to if they need help or have a problem.

Main activity: Make 'Helping hands'
Give each child a piece of coloured paper to draw round their hand. Then ask them to write the name of an adult they can talk to on each finger and cut it out to take home.

Make sure that you tell them they can always come to you and tell you what is worrying them. Remind pupils though that there may be times when you will need to pass their worries on to other people. Some teachers have a 'worry box' for children to communicate with them or set up a special time (bubble time for example) when children know they can come and talk.

Reflection/plenary
Pass the teddy bear/puppet around the class asking children to complete the sentence, 'If I were puppet/teddy I would speak to …' Pass a smile or hand squeeze round the class.

Differentiation
- *Children needing more of a challenge* – could work in twos to make up a play using two puppets, taking one of the examples from the main activity section.
- *Children with additional learning needs* – could do further role play with the puppet, explaining that it is alright to ask for help and suggesting people who could help.

What if …
- *A child discloses that a family member has been touching them inappropriately?* Follow up on the working agreement by saying that this is something the child could talk to you about in private after the lesson. Find a time to talk to them as soon as possible, praise them for being brave enough to tell you, do not promise confidentiality, and say you will try to get someone to help them. Follow the school's child protection procedures.
- *A child does not live with their parents?* Make sure that children who do not live with their parents still feel included by suggesting a wide range of people they could go to for help including their carers.

Someone to talk to (Key Stage 2)

By the end of this lesson pupils will be able to listen to and support others, identify adults they can trust and who they can ask for help, listen to and support their friends, and know where individuals, families and groups can get help.

Learning outcomes
- I can identify a range of situations where I might need help and I know where to go to get help.
- I know who I can talk to if I am upset/worried/anxious.
- I can identify people in my support network.
- I can identify people who can help me with different problems.
- I can help support someone who is unhappy or needs advice.

Working agreement
Remind the children about the working agreement and emphasise the importance of listening to each other, and that if they have any worries they can come and talk to you after the class.

Resources needed
- Flip chart or whiteboard
- Situations for Double Circles activity.

Opening activity: Listening pairs
Invite the children to form pairs. Tell one half of each pair (A) that they will be asked to talk about their favourite TV programme for a minute. Tell the other half of each pair (B), in private, that their partner will talk about their favourite TV programme for a minute and, they should look away, fidget, frown and repeat of a daft phrase to show they are not paying full attention.

Then ask the children to swap roles, explain what they now have to do and repeat the activity. Reflect on how the poor listening makes people feel; particularly if they had been trying to tell you something important. How could they show their partner that they are listening?

Then get the children to think about: how to talk to someone who confides in them; how they might be feeling; how they can be a good listener. Together, come up with a list of qualities of a good, supportive listener.

Main activity: Double circles
Ask the pairs, A and B, to form two circles, with As in the inner circle and their partner B facing them in the outer circle. Ask pairs to discuss what would you say or do if your friend said he/she was being bullied? Then ask the people on the outside to move one place to their left to stand opposite a new partner. Give a new situation to discuss. For example, what would you say or do if:

- Your friend said they were sad because their Dad has gone away?
- Your friend said they were feeling very worried about going on to secondary school?
- Your friend said she had started her period in school?
- Your friend told you that somebody in the playground had touched a private part of her body?

When the pupils have had the opportunity to discuss a range of situations with several partners, ask them to identify all the different sources of help for problems of different kinds.

Talk about how we can help each other – you may have a peer-mentoring or buddy scheme at the school, so be sure to mention this.

Reflection/plenary

Ask children to complete the sentence, 'If I had a problem I would talk to …'

Differentiation

- *Children needing more of a challenge* – could make up their own problems; develop this into a newsletter of the examples children feel are the most common. The teacher would edit this and then deliver it to all Key Stage 2 classrooms.
- *Children with additional learning needs* – could make a 'Time to listen' board. Each child or pair write something in a bubble for the board, such as: 'Don't butt in!', 'Be kind!', 'Smile!' or 'Remember your body language.' Suggest others who may be able to help.

Home work/Activity with parents

Talk about all the different kinds of people you can go to if you need help – friends, family members, professionals (school nurse, GP, social worker), those manning helplines, as well as those accessible via the internet.

Ask children to create their own personal directory of people they could talk to if they were worried about something, with phone numbers, email and web addresses, or where they can be found. For example:

Mum at work 0923 740937
Nan (Mrs XXX) 48239–58
School nurse (name) in the medical room on Tuesdays
Learning mentor in the staffroom on XXXX
ChildLine 0800 1111
Best friend 0922 928474.

They could add other types of sources of information and help to this, including websites that have been checked by the teacher. Use this as an opportunity to build on learning in other lessons about e-safety and taking care with searches that they do. They could make this into a little card or booklet that they could keep in their school bag. (If you have laminating facilities in school, it might be possible to make the booklets more durable.)

What if ...

A child should become upset and tearful in the lesson when they are talking about things that have made them sad? You may want to take them out and get someone (administrative staff, learning support assistant) to be with them until you can attend to them after the lesson. Alternatively, you may decide it can be handled in the classroom if you judge that the situation behind the behaviour may not be serious enough to warrant further exploration. You may decide, in fact, that it could be handled very well by the friends of the child concerned.

Sample assessment activities

Learning outcome	Assessment activity
I can give good advice about who can help if a child is sad or worried.	Show pictures of children looking sad or worried. Ask the children to identify and draw or write two people they would advise that child to talk to. Use teaching assistants to support less able children with this task. Collect in the work the children have done and identify if they are working towards, at or beyond the level expected. Or create a poster of who and how to access trusted adults.
• I can use listening skills to support others. • I can give advice. • I know where to go for extra help and support.	Children generate a list of success criteria for what giving good advice is. Put children into groups and ask them to role play giving advice to a friend or friends. (The teacher should provide scenarios based on issues that could be related to that age group.) The role plays are then shown to the rest of the class. The rest of the class assesses each role play according to the success criteria for giving good advice that have been generated.

References

Blake, S and Muttock, S (2012) *Assessment, Evaluation and Sex and Relationships Education: A Practical Guide for Education, Health and Community Settings*, 2nd ed. London: National Children's Bureau.

Blake, S and Power, P (2003) *Teaching and Learning About HIV: A Resource for Key Stages 1 to 4*. London: National Children's Bureau.

Department for Education and Employment (2000) *Sex and Relationships Education Guidance*. London: DfEE (0116/2000).

Department for Education and Skills (2005) *Excellence and Enjoyment: Social and Emotional Aspects of Learning (SEAL)*. London: DfES.

fpa/Mori (2000) *Sex Education Lessons for Parents From fpa*. http://www.ipsos-mori.com/ (accessed 20 July 2012).

Goleman, DP (1995) *Emotional Intelligence: Why it Can Matter More Than IQ for Character, Health and Lifelong Achievement*. London: Bantam Books.

Home Office (2010) *Call to End Violence Against Women and Girls*. London: Home Office.

Ingham, R and van Zessen, G (1998) *From Cultural Contexts to Interactional Competencies: A European Comparative Study*. An invited paper presented at 'AIDS in Europe: Social and Behavioural Dimensions', Paris 12–16 January 1998.

Lord Laming (2009) *The Protection of Children in England: Progress Report*. London: The Stationery Office.

Margetts, D and Lynch, M (2004) 'Fun without fear', *Spotlight*, 4, November, 10–11.

mumsnet (2011) mumsnet Sex Education Survey. www.mumsnet.com/campaigns/mumsnet-sex-education-survey#Results (accessed 6 September 2012)

National Society (2002) *Educating Children and Young People in School About Marriage*. London: Church House Publishing.

Office for Standards in Education (2002) *Sex and Relationships: A Report From Her Majesty's Chief Inspector of Schools* (HMI 433). London: Ofsted.

Office for Standards in Education (2012) *The Framework for School Inspection from January 2012* (ref 090019). London: Ofsted.

Papadopoulos, L (2010) *Sexualisation of Young People Review*. London: Home Office.

PSHE Association (2011) *Assessment in Secondary PSHE Education: Progression Framework for Planning and Assessment in PSHE Education*. London: The PSHE Association.

PSHE Association (2012) *PSHE Education and the New Ofsted Inspection Framework January 2012*. http://www.pshe-association.org.uk/uploads/media/17/7611.pdf (accessed 20 July 2012).

Qualifications and Curriculum Authority (1999a) *The National Curriculum Handbook for Primary Teachers in England*. London: Qualifications and Curriculum Authority.

Qualifications and Curriculum Authority (1999b) *The Standards Site: Science at Key Stages 1 and 2*. http://www.standards.dfes.gov.uk/schemes2/science/?view=get (accessed 29 November 2012)

Sex Education Forum (2004) *Faith, Values and Sex and Relationships Education: Forum Factsheet*. London: National Children's Bureau.

Sex Education Forum (2005) *Sex and Relationships Education Framework*. London: SEF.

Sex Education Forum (2006) *Call for PSHE, Which Includes Sex and Relationships Education, To Be Made Statutory*. London: National Children's Bureau.

Sex Education Forum (2010) *Understanding Sex and Relationships Education*. London: National Children's Bureau.

Sex Education Forum (2013) Let's Get it Right – A toolkit for involving primary school children in reviewing SRE. London: National Children's Bureau.

Sex Education Forum (2013) Let's work together – A practical guide for schools to involve parents and carers in SRE. London: National Children's Bureau.

Sample letter to parents of Key Stage 1 or Key Stage 2 children

Below is a sample of a letter you can send to parents of Key Stage 1 or 2 to accompany an overview of the lessons in this pack and ideas for their involvement, for example a book to read at home.

Dear ....,

I am writing to let you know that, over the next [insert number] of weeks, starting next [insert date], your child's class will be taking part in some Personal, Social and Health Education lessons which will include Sex & Relationships Education.

This is part of the whole-school Personal, Social & Health Education programme that is taught right through the school in every year and which is monitored and reviewed regularly by the staff and governing body.

Topics being taught to your child's class are:

- Male and female/body parts
- Growing and changing
- Similarities and differences
- Feelings
- Keeping safe
- Keeping yourself clean and healthy
- Someone to talk to
- Friends
- Families of all kinds
- Choices and consequences
- Gender stereotypes/Gender and sexuality.

You will have an opportunity to see the materials being used in the lessons including books and videos next ....[insert time/date]. You will also have the opportunity to find out how you can support your child with this topic at home.

If this date does not suit you, please contact your child's class teacher who will make arrangements to talk to you about the lessons.

Yours sincerely,

[Headteacher]

Appendix 2

Example questionnaire for parents and carers of primary age children (adapt to meet the needs of your setting)

Sex and Relationship Education at _____ *school*

We are currently reviewing our Sex and Relationship Education (SRE) Policy and curriculum and would like to involve parents and carers in this process as we recognise that the teaching of sex and relationships is a joint responsibility between home and school. Please tick the relevant boxes.

1. **Do you have a son or daughter at the school?**
   ☐ Daughter   ☐ Son   ☐ Both

2. **Are you aware of the school's current Sex and Relationship Education policy?**
   ☐ I have seen it   ☐ I have heard about it
   ☐ I do not know about it   ☐ I would like to know about it

3. **Would you like to be more involved in the review of the Sex and Relationship Education policy at our school?**
   ☐ Yes   ☐ Not sure   ☐ No

4. **Do you feel able to talk with your child or children about sexual matters, growing up and how to be safe?**
   ☐ Easily   ☐ Not very easily
   ☐ Depends on topic   ☐ Not at all

5. **What areas of Sex and Relationship education do you feel the school should cover?** *(Please state them)*

   _____

   _____

6. **Do you have any questions or concerns regarding your child's participation in the school's SRE programme?**
   ☐ Yes   ☐ No

7. **If Yes, please explain**

   _____

   _____

8. **Is there any support you would like from the school in talking to your child or children about Sex and Relationships?** *(Please state, although we may not be able to offer all the support requested.)*

   _____

   _____

Thank you for your help and we would like to invite you to a meeting to discuss this questionnaire and the development of sex and relationships education at our school. This meeting will take place on _____ at _____

Please indicate if you need any support to attend this meeting. For example, child care, translator, support accessing the building etc.